SOMEWHERE UNDER THE RAINBOW

Kelly L. Price & Jayce Kennedy Price

First Edition

ISBN:

Hardback: 978-1-950035-05-2

Paperback: 978-1-950035-03-8

eBook: 978-1-950035-04-5

Audiobook: 978-1-950035-06-9

Library of Congress Control Number 2021904130

Published in the United States by Blue Agama Books, 506 Peery Parkway, Golden, CO 80403

Editor: Cate Lockton Byers

Photography: Foxfish Photography

Cover Design: Joel A. Bass

Interior Layout: Michael Jenet, Journey Institute Press

Visit us on the Web at www.undertherainbowbook.com

Dedication

For Daniel, my amazing husband, jumping off cliffs with me for twenty years and still without a parachute.

Acknowledgements

None of this would have happened without Jayce Kennedy Price. He is an amazing kid who has taught me more and given me more than I could ever give him.

Daniel Price, whose question about where we would put Jayce pulled the wheel chock off the train and started it rolling.

The Kennedy family; Brian, Vivian, Isabelle, Charlie, and most of all Peter, for being amazing activists, advocates, and friends for all these years. We are lucky we know you.

The Pesce family, Tim, Michelle, Anna, and Chiara, who have gone above and beyond the call of duty in every instance to give Jayce, and by extension me, an extended family.

The Langhorst family, who are beloved friends and have been since our kids were little runts, and whose caring and generosity have carried me many times.

The Panzer family, who have taught me the value of connection and community.

My parents Dave and Linda Van Keuren, who once opened their home to my own childhood best friend when he was in crisis and scared and alone.

Kaiden Price, who never fails to say, "Can we adopt this one too?" when confronted with yet another potential Price kid.

Gabrielle Price, who understands unconditional love better than anyone I know and who captured Jayce perfectly for the cover of the Jayce File.

Mareille Price, whose wisdom and practicality have helped me see the world through new eyes ever since they arrived in our family.

Kari Cochran, for talking me off multiple ledges as this process unfolded.

TC McCracken, for comedy above and beyond the call of duty.

Emma Watson, for being inspiring. Or something.

Cate Byers, for editing, mentoring, and telling me the book was funny as hell at a time when I really needed that. You made this thing so much better.

Katy Snyder, for car theft, love, adventure, and for being the mom I channel when things get crazy.

Michael and Dafna Michaelson Jenet and the rest of the JI

Press writing group where people said, "Good job!"

Brianna Titone, for representation, catching pronoun errors, and facilitating critical connections.

And last but not least, Noodles & Company, for being the weirdest place to get another kid ever, as well as for all the garlic bread.

FOREWORD

by Brian Kennedy

There should be a massive difference between the consequences of substantial efforts aimed at righting wrongs and honoring commitments and the consequences of lame gestures via social media. Somewhere Under The Rainbow was actually made possible by one rather lame text message I wrote while riding the bus to the airport.

This message, one of many written on that fateful bus ride, was generated by an exhausted mind, seeking distractions from the burdens of work obligations. The message was sent with just a glimmer of hope that increased connection between one old friend and her family and one new friend, who had recently met in my home at a graduation party, might be good... Well, it is fair to say that the life-altering chain reaction that followed delivery of this message occurred at blinding speed and is still racing into a previously unimaginable future, and all of that was mighty good.

This chain reaction is at the heart of this book, but the kindnesses that preceded the lame text message and occurred thereafter are where the primary lessons can be learned and applied. This book is about the importance of every kindness and the healing power of laughter stuffed into the face of pain, fear, doubt, and uncertainty.

This book is not about lies and deception. This book is about the type of bonding between people that can occur when understanding and acceptance are front and center, allowing for lightheartedness even when looking back at a wide range of events that should never have occurred.

To know Kelly is to love Kelly. In fact, to really know someone is to understand and accept them, even if they are goofy as hell and would bite the head off someone who would harm a child. To know Daniel, now that is an entirely different matter. If you know Daniel, you are in an elite group. He stands firmly where his intellect and commitments place him and if you are patient and your own biases don't get in the way, he will open up and you will find him to be extremely intelligent, curious, eager to share ideas and remarkably fun. This introverted Ph.D. and extraordinary athlete is an inspiring and powerful counterpart to Kelly's often hilarious commentary and "take no prisoners" approach to righting wrongs.

When Kelly met Jayce, she certainly recognized goofy. She also saw an abundance of joy and creativity, his longing for connection and untapped potential. Underneath his exterior, Kelly recognized something raw and hurting. Somewhere Under The Rainbow is the story of the love between a fierce Mama Bear and an injured cub and how they find ways to joke their way through some serious stuff and some not so serious stuff.

Life would be simple if people were all the same. It would also be as boring as hell. The characters in this story are unusual folk, in the best possible ways. This family has an amazing capacity to love and give to all around them.

As you read this book, imagine your own resilience under these circumstances, and think about what you might do.

These parents right wrongs and fulfill honorable commitments. They love unconditionally and act accordingly. They are also as funny as hell. Jayce and his story affirm our hopes and dreams that people care, heal, and respond well to kindness and the right type of silliness.

Brian Kennedy

Chapter 1

Meet the Prices

Thank you for joining us on this crazy journey.

Disclaimer: This book is not actually a guide to much of anything. There are going to be some tips, tricks and thoughts sprinkled throughout, but the main purpose Jayce and I had in telling our story was to entertain. Maybe the ideas in here will make you more comfortable with the trans community, who after all, are just people. Maybe you're parenting, supporting, or mentoring a trans kid yourself and need some ideas or need to feel like you're connected to a bigger community and are not alone. Maybe you ARE a trans kid living with the physical, psychological, and social ramifications of being transgender in today's society and you just want to be able to laugh about life a little bit with someone who is there with you. We're game. We'll walk the road with you and listen to your thoughts about your own journeys and provide a little camaraderie for you, or shed a little light on the realities of day to day life as a trans guy (or in my case as the parent of a trans guy.) We'll also make you laugh.

Note this book is written mainly from the perspective of the transgender male teen, or rather, from that of his mom. For clarity, someone who was assigned the female gender at birth based on anatomy, and who later transitions to male is a transgender man. Someone who was assigned the male gender at birth based on anatomy, and who later transitions to female, is a transgender woman. Trans men are men, period. Trans women are women, period. Since Jayce is a trans man, neither he nor I have a lot of insider experience on the care and keeping of trans women (or agender, or nonbinary, or genderfluid, or genderqueer, or whichever thing you identify with) folks. I haven't parented or supported a transgender girl before, so we won't be speaking much about that experience. We can make semi-educated guesses about some of things they might experience, but that's about the best we can offer. Also, we are trying very hard to be conversant with current and correct language being used to describe the people and events in the book. Missteps and misidentifications in this respect are more likely to be mine than Jayce's, but rest assured we'll clean it all up the best we can and try to discuss issues with care, kindness, and humor.

Another note for you: we totally get that a lot of traumatic stuff happens to people in the trans community. We are not aiming to belittle or invalidate ANYONE with this work. We just want to tell our story from a somewhat lighthearted point of view.

The last disclaimer here is that if profanity, discussion of body-related topics, or discussion of sexual functioning offends you terribly… this is not the book for you. Sometimes it's because we are seeking to inject some humor into some difficult situations and occasionally we get a little crude, and other times it's necessary to describe things with clarity and precision.

This book covers roughly the first year after Jayce joined our family. It was a year of highs and lows, rearrangements and reprioritizations, and a lot of love.

I'm a nurse, a wife, and a suburban Mama Bear. My kids are my highest priority; my life is dedicated to ensuring that they thrive. I have backgrounds in public health nursing, special needs care, and hospice care as well as in education. I am, if I do say so myself, a hell of a good advocate for people whose voices, for whatever reason, are stilled or muffled. On top of that I am an extreme extrovert and I have amazing friends. I can network like a CEO. I know people in local and state politics, people attached to community resources, and people who are just generally fabulous humans.

In the summer of 2018, my husband Daniel and I were living with our three kids in suburban Denver, minding our own business. Part of that business was vocal advocacy for the LGBTQ community. Two of our three kids at that time fit in "somewhere under the rainbow" with one transgender son who is pansexual, one cisgender daughter, and one nonbinary first grader. We did not know at that time that any of the Price kids were gender quirky, we thought we had three girls, but as they've explored their own identities they have changed things.

I'll get to that.

A few weeks prior to meeting Jayce I got myself involved with a group on Facebook called Free Mom Hugs. The point of the group is fairly self-explanatory, I think. It all started with a wonderful lady named Sara Cunningham whose son came out to her as gay and who had to make a journey from a place of nonacceptance to a place of affirmation if she was going to maintain a relationship with her child. She processed that whole journey by writing a book. It is called *How We Sleep At Night: A Mother's Memoir* (Createspace Independent Publishing Platform, 2014) and it is an extraordinary work of soul-searing clarity that describes her emotional journey as a Christian.

Free Mom Hugs members show up to Pride events and hug people, literally. In many cases it's just a hug but in some it's badly needed, because LGBTQ kids are often ostracized by their own parents and exiled from the communities that were supposed to support them. Mom huggers hear things like, "My own mom hasn't hugged me in three years" and, "I got kicked out of my house when I came out as trans, I don't know where my mom even is now." If you're a Free Mom Hugs volunteer you open your arms wide and give these people a hug exactly like one you'd give your own child, and you tell them they are perfect and loved exactly the way they are. The Moms go home covered in glitter and streaked with tears and then go back and do it again at the next event.

The statistics on LGBTQ kids are sobering. Approximately one in four eventually loses their home. 41% of transgender kids eventually attempt suicide. They are more likely to be trafficked, end up as sex workers, be victims of familial abuse, and engage in self-destructive and self-harming behaviors like cutting and drug abuse. They are less likely to receive higher education, often due to the loss of parental support they experience.

Also, there is zero empirical evidence showing that any intervention whatsoever can alter a person's gender identity or sexual orientation. Zero. Nada. Every piece of legitimate science we have seems to show that all aspects of gender, biological sex, and sexual orientation are laid down in utero or in very early childhood. It's not possible to 'convert' someone, although it IS possible to hurt them enough so that they won't ACT on their attractions. It likewise is not possible to 'pray the gay away'. I'm not going to cite sources here or quote from scholarly analyses about these things; if you need an education it is readily available. I would begin with GLAAD (the Gay And Lesbian Alliance Against Defamation) or PFLAG (Parents and Friends of Lesbians and Gays) or even the Gay-Straight Alliance coordinator at your local high school.

My husband, Daniel, has been an extremely dedicated educator for ages and ages and has a doctorate. He teaches chemistry at the high school level and is also qualified to do math and physics. He grades student work the same day it gets submitted and hands it back to the kids the next class period with individual sticky notes on each paper that say what they got wrong and what they need to do to fix it, which they then get to do for full credit. He notices things in a way that people often underestimate—just about the time you think he isn't paying attention, it turns out that yes, he is.

He's also got a rock-solid sense of integrity that says you do what's right in this life or you don't get to look yourself in the mirror and sleep at night with a clear conscience. This would probably qualify him for a career in politics except for the fact that he's an introvert who sequesters himself in a distant room in front of a computer when there are too many people around. In a family that now contains four kids, there are always too many people around. He insists that it be noted that he is NOT a hugger and never will be. The ways he shows love are based in action – he'll donate, use his time, help advocate, act as a sounding board, and think his way around problems that I tend to try to hammer through. We make an incredibly good team and have for 21 years now, so we must be doing something right.

We have three other kids, and this is where the pronouns will get weird, so get ready to wrap your brains around part of my world. The pronouns get weird for reasons that will become clear as we go on.

Kaiden, who is now 18, was born fourteen weeks premature and weighed in at a whopping one pound and four ounces (and lost those four ounces after birth.) Kaiden was a tiny, feisty, fiery little baby with a tendency to yank out his breathing tubes and create havoc in the neonatal intensive care unit where he stayed for 129 days, nine hours, and fifteen minutes (not that anyone was counting.) He was resuscitated 240 times, had a feeding tube until age 12, got repeated pneumonias as a little kid, and required hundreds of hours of therapy. Kaiden is now a passionate and articulate advocate for kids with disabilities as well as for the LGBTQ community, and like that guy on the old Hair Club For Men commercials, is also a member; identifying as pansexual and transgender male. Kaiden's pronouns are "He, Him, and His."

Kaiden is a whole lot tougher than he appears. He will cry if hurting or stressed or angry, but then come back steelier than ever. If you've got this kid on your side you have one of the most loyal, patient, and loving people in your court that you could ever want. He has a generous nature that knocks me out. When we got his youngest sibling Mari in the most sudden and surprising way possible (yes, we had an accidental adoption) he said, "Oh yay, Mama, can we adopt this one too?"

Gabrielle is 12 and is a sixth grader whose entire life has been filled with protests and social justice action. One of her very first battle cries was, "We! Are! The 99%!" and she hollered this from my shoulders with tiny little fist pumps and an enthusiasm that nearly unseated her. She was also a preemie, born fifteen weeks early and very, very sick, and she spent six months in intensive care at Children's Hospital of Colorado before transitioning to medical foster care and from there to us at just over a year of age. She still has her feeding tube and some delays, but her determination and tenacity have ensured that she's reading at grade level, walks, talks, climbs things, and creates chaos every bit as well as her siblings do. She recently got involved in the campaign for Representative Brianna Titone, who ran for and won herself a State House seat in Colorado House District 27. Brianna is the second openly transgender representative at the state level in US history, and she ran an incredibly tight and classy grassroots campaign in a district that usually goes for the Republican candidates by double digits. Gabi stamped postcards and painted our car with window markers so the campaign would be supported in style by having its message emblazoned on a battered blue minivan known to us as Priscilla, Queen Of The Suburbs. She also wrote a letter to Rep. Titone when somebody in the opposing campaign was using her old, or 'dead' name;

Dear Brianna,

I am sorry you are being deadnamed. That is mean. When you win your election we will take you out for ice-cream.

Love Gabi.

She's smart, funny, sarcastic, and one of the most caring kids I know. Her pronouns are "She, Her, and Hers."

Mari is the third of my brace of badass babies. They are eight, a third-grader who reads at roughly a seventh-grade level, and this child doesn't miss a thing. Mari came to us when we got a call out of the clear blue sky in May of 2012 from Social Services saying, "Hi, we need emergency placement for Gabi's biological baby sibling, are you interested? Oh and don't leave, I don't know when they'll be there." A few hours later a harried social worker showed up, handed me a shrieking eight-week-old baby, and left without even making me sign anything. Fourteen months later we finalized Mari's adoption in a courtroom with a bemused judge who watched them clambering eagerly up and down the various risers and steps in the courtroom and decided they'd be all right with us.

Mari is analytical, fierce as hell, and perfectionistic. Like their father, Mari holds theirself to very high standards in almost everything they do, with the possible exceptions of cleaning and putting away clothes. Mari will occasionally just decide in school that they're not doing whatever the assigned task is, making their teacher crazy. I think someday they'll have a lot of T-shirts and bumper stickers that say things like *Question Authority,* and *I Think, Therefore I'm Dangerous.* In spite of their teacher's protests, I don't have a whole lot of problems with this. I anticipate that Mari will be utterly impervious to peer pressure as a teenager, so I am highly motivated to get them to use their stubbornness and creativity for good purposes as an adult. I do not doubt for a single second their capacity to accomplish anything they set out to do.

Mari is also very accepting of the quirks of other people. Like the other kids before them, they have friends who have disabilities, challenges, and wildly differing political upbringings, and they meet them all with their own special Mari brand of tolerance and matter of fact acceptance. When Jayce has panic attacks or trauma flashbacks, looking at Mari really helps, because there was no Mari in his old life so logically he can't still be there. Mari is the self-described 'Jaycequake, Trauma, Panic And Flashback Assistant'. They made a name tag. Mari identifies as nonbinary, and pronouns are "They, Them, and Their."

Into this mishmash we now introduce Jayce.

———

18

He is 21 years old, the son I did not know I needed until he was here. He is a junior in college, an accomplished and talented musician, brilliantly intelligent, and possessed of a naturally sweet nature and sunny disposition that has withstood years of adversity and challenges. He joined our family in October of 2018, and it is as though he has always been here. Oh, and in case I hadn't mentioned it before this, Jayce is transgender.

Jayce gets weirded out when things seem too normal. He gets himself all in a dither over needing to address some concern that then turns out to be not that bad. He's used to conversations about serious topics ending with somebody screaming at or hitting him, which isn't happening here, so he's a little bit at loose ends when we need to deal with some issue and all that happens is a discussion and then stuff gets solved.

So, consider yourselves introduced. And buckle up because it's about to get crazy. We'll keep it real for you as we go along.

Meet Jayce

Growing up, I actually considered myself a pretty typical kid. I was born in Kemerovo, Russia, adopted from an orphanage there, and brought to the United States at 2 years old. I was told that I was born with meningitis and hospitalized for a year. I don't know how accurate that was, but doctors apparently didn't expect me to survive. They believed that if I did, I wouldn't walk, speak, hear, see... I'd pretty much be disabled. However, I defied medical expectations because anyone who knows me at all, knows that I do not shut up. I happened to recover from whatever my condition was and now, you would never know.

Anyhow, when I was brought to Colorado, I believed I had a fairly good life. I was thankful to have been chosen by a family and I thought I was cared for. Maybe it began that way.

I grew up as a child that would never stop moving. I was a dancer for the majority of my life, as well as an athlete all year around. Don't ask me how I had time to sleep because the truth is, I have no idea. Believe it or not, I was considered a goody-two-shoes, perfectionist, introverted, and shy kid. Again, if you know me, you wouldn't be able to imagine, but that's who I was.

In the early years I would always try so hard to be perfect, make sure I followed the rules to the last detail and make sure you did too. I was intelligent beyond my years and would be talking about philosophy to my grandmother when I was 8 years old. I had a talent for writing poetry and would enjoy drawing for hours at a time. When I think about it, the quiet perfectionist persona came from the pressure I felt at home. I was expected to maintain ridiculous academic and social standards and I really was never encouraged to speak up for myself. I was raised to keep my mouth shut.

From my perspective, my life was normal, but as I grew older, I began to realize that things were slowly starting to go downhill. I recall when I was about 11, my father and I exchanged our first insults at home, something we never had done before. But he made it into a game and taught me that that was how I could behave.

I was told by my mother that no one liked me and everyone was watching me and laughing behind my back. So, my self-confidence wasn't great. Near the end of middle school, however, I started to find out who I really was, which was an extremely extroverted, creative, friendly, social person that was easy to get along with. As the emotional abuse increased in severity and the home environment became violent, I found a new voice and confidence that I didn't know was there. I'm not a shy person naturally. I was scared. There was fear in my eyes daily.

I stopped hiding and found power in dance and songwriting. I continued to grow up and I was still invalidated. I would avoid being at home as often as I could. I would pick up extra shifts at work so I didn't have to come home early, I'd make money to feed myself a few nights at a time, and then when I had to, I would return home and shut down. I'd spend my weekends outside all day. Anywhere but at home.

When I came out as transgender at 17, nothing got easier. I was abused in every way and backed into a corner constantly. My only choice was to find things and people to keep me going. I was told I would not get any treatment for gender care until I was 25 and could not move out until my parents decided I was ready. They had a special talent for flipping every disaster on me, so I legitimately thought that I'd find myself in jail at 16. Turns out, after pushing through for so many years, my life finally came together and I was everything my former parents told me I would never be.

Chapter 2

Kelly: Restaurants

The roof of the restaurant parted company from the I-beam that had held it up for nearly three decades with an enormous crunching sound that shook the world. The excavator looked like some sort of prehistoric predator, gnashing and lurching its way through the demolition site with enormous steel teeth.

Jayce waved his chicken wing in the air.

"OH yeah!" he hollered joyfully through a mouthful of buffalo sauce. "THERE it is! This is the best mother-son bonding experience EVER!" This was high praise.

We were sitting in my van outside the drugstore in early spring of 2020, watching the death of the restaurant. I owed Jayce buffalo wings as compensation for driving his siblings to school. Buffalo wings are considered by him to be the absolute pinnacle of what he calls Dude Food, and he has a point. There is no way to eat these things with gentility or dignity. Whatever sauce you pick ends up liberally spattered across your face as you rip the meat off the bones with your teeth. I've been a mom for a long time though, and I had napkins.

It was hard to envision a more utterly macho day for a transgender son than sitting in a van eating Dude Food after picking up your testosterone prescription and watching people literally smash a building to matchsticks. We had a great time, taking videos and pictures, whooping and applauding when an especially noisy or large event of destruction occurred, eating our wings and ignoring the celery stalks and carrot sticks served with them. We watched the demolition with rapt joy for nearly an hour and a half, enjoying the sunshine, the crash and tinkle of Restaurantgeddon across the parking lot, and our own dorkiness. There were four perfectly lined up barstools that had been carefully placed just inside the construction fence for some unknown reason, and we had fun conjecturing about whether those were the cheap seats or the expensive ones.

Some of the pivotal pieces of our tale involve restaurants. Here is another.

You can get some really bizarre things off-menu at Noodles & Company. I like that pasta fresca thing they do that has noodles and balsamic vinegar and cheese. It's got a sort of sophisticated flavor profile that Jayce would refer to as 'elevated'. Some place on the menu it says it's halfway healthy, too, which makes me feel good about eating the garlic bread. Not eating the garlic bread is unthinkable.

That garlic bread is heavenly death on a little black plastic plate. It has just the right amount of crust and buttery, garlicky goodness and they give you this little dish of marinara sauce to dip it in that rocks it to a new level. Of course, I'm no connoisseur when it comes to food, anything that somebody else cooks tends to taste pretty good to me. I have to admit, though, I didn't expect to go to Noodles & Company and end up with another kid.

I'm eccentric in that I like teenagers. This is my favorite age to parent so far. My kids tend to be a bit on the quirky side, so their friends are truly entertaining people. Kaiden's group of friends from elementary and middle school refers to themselves as the Radioactive Hamsters and they are a hilarious bunch of sarcastic pranksters who slip from trash-talking over a pool game, to playing role-play games at lunch at school, to debating whether Western media has poisoned the views Americans hold of government systems in Syria or China. They have tons of energy, eat me out of house and home, and drive my poor, peace-loving, introverted husband totally bonkers. Daniel usually bails out and heads for the bedroom, or if he can, leaves the house altogether.

Among our family friends we include the Kennedy family; we've known them for twenty years. Brian and his wife Vivian have three kids, and all their lives they've been dynamic activists for cystic fibrosis research, and avid athletes, and generally cool people. Their kids are officially now all grown, a thing I admit to being a tad jealous of.

Peter, their youngest, befriended Jayce over a bike ride during their high school careers, and they hung out together and did teenager things. They both graduated in spring of 2018, and when Peter's parents threw him a graduation party at their house in Boulder, they invited us. They have a huge yard and they had set up all manner of outdoor games for people to play at the party.

So, the whole Price family piled into the van and went to their house, and while we were there, we met this teenager. He was a quirky, extroverted, engaging kid with a quick wit and a willingness to socialize with random strangers. He had only begun a social gender transition at that point, but to my eyes he was clearly male, and everyone else at the party seemed to treat him as male also. I did think he looked very young for a new high school graduate, but my experience with my gifted kids caused me to label him as possibly having skipped a grade due to giftedness. He was small, lithe, and graceful, with glasses and a fast walk.

We decided that since we were outdoors, we were kind of obligated to go play some of the games and so we started with badminton.

Well, let me tell you about my natural athletic ability. I haven't got any. I'm about as coordinated as a spider on LSD. Go find those videos where the spider gets drugs and makes a web that is totally outside the rules of geometry and everyone laughs at it. You will sit around wondering what spider hallucinations look like.

I do not understand the pursuit of balls in any sport. What is this fascination with getting and keeping this small round piece of inflated leather or rubber or whatever? Why must we put it in the little hoop? Why do we care if it goes in the little net? Why, for the love of Pete, do we need to physically tackle one another to get it back?

Okay, now picture a spider tripping on LSD and holding a badminton racquet and you've got a pretty good mental image of me playing sports.

The teams were selected and we were off. Team A consisted of four Prices. Me, Kaiden, Gabi, and Mari, all on one side of the net.

Team B consisted of Jayce. Just Jayce, all by himself, occupying one whole side. Team Price got absolutely annihilated. The dude would lay out like Superman to get a shot back and then somehow get back up and over to the other side in time to hit back whatever was coming his way. We, on the other side, couldn't hit these things back if we tried, which we really didn't. There were four of us on our badminton team, and when the birdie came across the net we'd all yell, "Yours!" and let it drop harmlessly between us into the grass, whereupon Jayce would do this little fist pump and go, "Yesssss!" like there was Olympic caliber glory in clobbering four spiders on acid. So, I decided to do what any normal, sane person should do under such circumstances. I switched teams and defected to Jayce's side. I sold my children completely up the river for a badminton birdie and the right to say I was on a winning team. And then I proceeded to stand there and let him do all the work, because it's just better for everyone that way and I was willing to make the sacrifice. I'm good like that.

It was, of course, a bloodbath, and of course Jayce and I won because of my extraordinary support, and I got credited with an assist and then there was food. We went to eat and he kept hanging out with us, talking to Kaiden and generally being an agreeable guy, and then it was time to congratulate Peter and go home.

Kaiden wanted me to ask Brian for Jayce's contact info so maybe the two of them could hang out on Instagram or something sometime. I got that info, and that was the end of it. Or so I believed, because on that day, remaining a three-child family seemed a foregone conclusion.

Fast forward to the middle of October, 2018. I was sitting with my family eating dinner; I forget if it was Applebee's or Ruby Tuesday but one of those generic chain places guaranteed to have some kind of mac and cheese or nugget-shaped food to keep the younger kids appeased. My phone pinged at me. The message was from Brian.

"Did you and Jayce ever connect?"

I messaged him back with, "No, we didn't. I liked that kid, how is he?"

"Not too good right now," came the reply. "His home life is tough and he's got parents who don't accept him."

Accept him for what? I wondered. I hadn't even thought about Jayce's gender identity when we met him. He was just a boy. Then I thought back to the party, remembering the small, graceful boy I had met, and the light dawned. Brian sees the stuff I post on social media and a lot of it has to do with being an LGBTQ ally. Ohhhh. Right. Duh. "So is he trans?" I asked, and got an answer in the affirmative. I thought about it for a minute and then asked what Brian needed me to do for Jayce.

"He could use another adult friend," wrote Brian. "Somebody who can just offer him some support and encouragement as he goes through college."

Okay, I thought, I can do that. I accepted Jayce's contact info again and tapped out a quick message.

"Hi," I wrote, "Brian thought maybe you could use some support and a friend, can I take you to lunch sometime next week?" I added a recap of the time we spent together at Peter's grad party and reassured him that I wasn't some random weirdo, but rather a weirdo well known to Brian and Vivian. This, combined with the offer of food, caused him to decide maybe lunch would work.

"I suppose you know I'm trans," he texted. I confirmed that yes, I was aware of this. We both looked at calendars and a plan was formulated. Jayce and I decided to get together on a fateful Tuesday at Noodles & Company.

I got there a little bit early and hung out until Jayce arrived. He arrived nearly on time, walking quickly across the parking lot, and we spent a few minutes reminiscing about the grad party and making small talk. We ordered food and went to a table and I asked one question of him:

"Are you safe at home?"

Well, that question opened up a huge can of worms. You know those giant-size jars of mayonnaise you can get at Costco? That was the size of that can of worms. We could have stocked a bait shop for a year, and it became clear very quickly that he was absolutely not safe at home. The floodgates opened and Jayce started talking, and the picture he painted included physical and emotional abuse and complete disregard for his gender issues, and so when I could get a word in edgewise I blurted out, "What if you had someplace to go? Some way to get out of there?" He allowed as to how that would be most welcome and I thought "Well, here we go," and I messaged Daniel.

"We need to talk about Jayce, dear."

Daniel knew about the lunch plan and the message from Brian, and he knows me very well. To his everlasting credit, and because he is a truly good guy, he had a single question:

"So are we moving Gabi and Mari in together or repurposing the office?"

Jayce: Noodles & New Starts

Now that I look back on the experience of eating wings and watching a restaurant get torn down with my mom, it's the kind of moment I never thought I would get to experience in my lifetime because of where I came from. We were just sitting there laughing like idiots and eating hot wings and having a good time. It was the kind of day I wish I'd had more of, growing up.

It's important to know that I came from an unaccepting household for the first eighteen years of my life. I never really had too much in common with my former adoptive parents. They never really understood me, didn't understand the things I would do for fun. It was kind of all about them having their way. It didn't feel right. I was hoping to make it out of that home, that it would come to an end and I could get out, get on my feet like everyone does. It took a while.

Here is a key bit of information that makes this book what it is in the first place. I am female to male transgender. That means I was born in the body of a female and I transitioned to male. I live my life as male because my brain is male. I came out as trans at seventeen, and it just created more problems than I could even count.

While I was going through my early transition, I met one of my closest friends, Peter Kennedy, while we were in high school. We've been best friends for many years now. I was invited to his graduation party in the summer of 2018 and that's quite literally when my life changed. I had no idea at the time.

At that party I met Kelly Price, our author (and my mom now). She and Daniel, my dad, had three kids of various ages. When I met them Mari was six, Gabi was nine, and Kaiden was fifteen. Being the outgoing person that I am, I was eager to get out in the yard and play badminton at the graduation party, and Kelly and her kids were up for joining me. I had a lot of fun making fun of them, winning, and bragging about it (which I still do to this day). It seemed like a completely normal evening.

One thing I noticed immediately about this mother was that she simply allowed her kids to be kids. She let them run around, play, it didn't matter if they could hit the ball or not. She accepted them. This was something I never had, so even though it just seemed to be in a minor context like letting your kid play sports, it was still big for me.

I left the party, and I vaguely remember Kaiden wanting my contact info but I never followed up on that. Apparently Brian, Peter's dad, did.

In October of 2018 I had recently begun college. I was trying to learn how to juggle a difficult home life, attend classes, maintain academic good standing, and accept myself for being transgender. All these things were pretty difficult.

One night I got a text from Kelly Price. At this point in time I couldn't quite put the face to the name until she reminded me who she was. As soon as she did, it clicked. She was very friendly to reach out, and one of the first things I said was "I suppose you know I'm trans." Kelly confirmed this and I agreed to meet her the next Tuesday for lunch at Noodles & Company.

We all joke about the rewards program at Noodles & Company now, because of the events that followed.

I met Kelly on my lunch break that day, and I just thought I was going to get another adult friend, have some lunch, and life would go on exactly how it had been. Nothing would change. It turned out that was completely false and not even close.

We got to talking about my home life, and Kelly asked a question that changed my entire life, and her life too. She asked, "Are you safe?"

I replied with "Depends on the day." This was really the truth. I just would never know. Some days things were fine, and other days I was actively in danger in my old home. I never could predict how a given day would go.

I had come to terms with my awful circumstances at that point, so I saw no point in holding back, and I unloaded a variety of terrible stories onto Kelly to give her a better understanding of my situation. When I told her that my mother had said she would rather have me as a dead daughter than as a happy son, Kelly said "I'm ready to audition for the part of being your mother." I was secretly hoping that she WOULD become my mother.

She absolutely got the part. She was the ideal mother I had been hoping for as long as I could possibly remember.

Kelly checked with her husband Daniel pretty immediately, and he knew what would happen, because they'd done this before. I have to make it known that I credit him forever for only asking about bedroom arrangements, considering that they had just gotten themselves into a potentially really big mess. It was a huge commitment.

So, three days later, the chaos began, and this book covers the majority of that chaos. On that day I would never have thought, I would never have been able to tell you, that a lunch at Noodles & Company would lead me to the reality I have now. It was opening with the story that I was sitting in the parking lot with my mom, laughing and eating Dude Food, and truly feeling like this was always where I was meant to be.

Chapter 3
Kelly: It's In The Contract

After much consideration and much discussion—most of it over text—we decided it would be a good idea to have Jayce come over after work one night and hash out the details of what life in the Price household would look like for him. I got up at 3:30 in the morning (this will become a common theme in my life, I have had a lot of days that include two 3:30's recently) and sat in front of the computer and drafted a document that we all now refer to as The Contract. This thing is about three pages long and it reads like a set of rules for a kindergarten classroom. You know the kind of thing:

Respect others' property.

Keep hands and arms inside the vehicle at all times.

Do not ride this ride if you are pregnant or have back problems.

Okay so those last two aren't in there, but they probably should be because this trans-teen parenting thing is no roller coaster for the faint-hearted wussies among us. This thing is hardcore. Someone could literally lose an arm if they're not careful. Anyway, I drafted this document at 3:30 in the morning and everybody went, "Ooh, this stuff is all kind of based on common sense" and then we all signed and witnessed it, which brought us to Weirdness #1: The name issue. It seemed wildly wrong to have Jayce sign the document in his *legal* name, since at that time we didn't even KNOW his legal name. But… signing it with his chosen name would make it questionably legal. In the end I decided screw it, we'd just get it witnessed, and my mom did that for us, and a good time was had by all.

Common sense rules for living with a new family included the following: Park at the curb in front of the house and don't block people's driveways, expectations of reasonable privacy and property rules, access to common areas of the house and responsibility for helping maintain those areas, and nonviolent, kind conflict resolution techniques for when we all drive each other up the proverbial wall.

The trouble, of course, is that every agreement has loopholes. I did not, alas, put specifics into the contract about things like indoor chainsaw use and when/where to use a pickaxe. Possibly I should have done so, but so far, since I don't actually own a chainsaw or a pickaxe, we're good. I am not mentioning the leaf blower or the circular saw until I really have to.

So far, The Contract is working well as a guiding framework thingy. I don't think I need a bunch of Supreme Court caliber scholars to interpret the rules, and everyone is forever citing The Contract and reminding each other of its existence and contents ("You cannot allow dishes to overflow the world, it's in The Contract.")

Two days after we signed this amazing Constitutional document, we all got kind of irrationally panicky for some reason. We had this vague plan to get Jayce moved in with us in 'a few days' or 'early next week' and the plan didn't really include a lot of specific details, like what he'd be bringing along or how we'd be transporting it. I had no clue if we needed a truck, or what. Home Depot rents trucks for reasonably cheap, though, so I figured that was a good plan if we needed one.

Anyway, that Thursday night I texted Jayce and asked him how things were going at home and got back an answer that was vague, yet disturbing. "OK I guess. I am fine for tonight."

Fine for tonight. Hmm. What the heck, exactly, did that mean? Why that word, 'tonight'? What was up that meant he maybe wouldn't be fine for tomorrow?

I texted him back and asked if he wanted to start moving things out of there the next day, which was a Friday. He allowed that maybe that would be a good idea and I said I'd be in touch after I took the kids to school that Friday morning, like around 8:00.

Apparently the 'around 8:00' part didn't register. This would lead to considerable consternation for me on the following morning, which to our surprise turned out to be Moving Day.

Jayce: Sign Your Life Away

After I met Kelly at Noodles & Company, I still didn't quite know what the plan was, but I had a gut feeling that this might be my one chance to get out of the situation I was in. I had kept in contact with Kelly after our lunch that day. I still couldn't believe she was serious, that I was being given an offer to stay with her and her family for as long as it took to get me on my feet. The next three days after first discussing this were the most chaotic of my entire life. I still wasn't sure because I barely knew these people, but Kelly invited me over to dinner the next day to officially meet everyone. When I got there, I was presented with The Contract. This was essentially a document that just said, "I'll be respectful," like, they'll respect me and I'll respect them. Nothing there seemed unreasonable. Reading the agreement Kelly had drafted, I thought, "Wow, they are actually serious. Holy crap, this is real." So even though I hadn't thought much of this through, or really ANY of this through, I felt I had no choice but to make a decision on the fly. It all sounded pretty promising, so I signed the thing.

Later I was asked by Kelly, "Why did you trust us? We were basically complete strangers." The truth was that I believed I had no choice, and I also trusted Brian, Peter's dad. If he said they were good people, then the Prices were good people.

I was driving home after having signed this thing, and I literally couldn't believe what I had just done. I could not believe I had just signed myself over to another family, over pizza. Did I know what I was doing? Absolutely not. I did know

I had to jump and take this opportunity for myself. This was essentially a 'do or die' moment.

That night I happened to run into Brian in my neighborhood park. I was just hanging out by myself, trying to process everything that had just happened. He said, "You've heard about the offer, what do you think?" and I responded with "I can't believe anybody wants me."

Brian joined me on a walk and offered to talk things through with me. We were talking about trying to do some damage control, because we both knew my parents were not going to take this well at all. It was essentially going to be a disaster. We talked about having me transition into this situation slowly, maybe by spending a couple of days a week at the Prices' house, but there was just no way to do that without drawing out the process and allowing more time for abuse.

After I walked and talked with Brian, I brought the contract home to my parents. I wasn't planning on showing them, but I said "I've been given an offer. I have a place to go, and I'm leaving."

This was followed by screaming and violence. Their reaction was absolute proof of why I needed to accept this offer. At that point I knew it was right. I had no idea what was gonna happen, but I knew I had made the decision to the best of my ability. I recognized that the Prices' offer was what I needed.

My parents screamed at me. They screamed "Do you even know what you're doing? Because you can't come back when this fails."

"No, I don't. But anywhere is better than here."

They responded, again screaming, "So when are you leaving?"

I said, "Probably sometime next week."

It turned out that was not the case. I left two days later.

Chapter 4

Kelly: Refreshments For Cult Meetings

If you're unfamiliar with teenagers, you don't know what they're like in the morning. Like vampires, kind of, except less focused on their goals and more likely to crumble to dust in sunlight. They make inarticulate noises at you if you disturb them and they won't remember anything you told them the day before. You can literally go through every detail of a plan in the evening with your teenager's full undying attention and when you remind them of Step 1 of that same plan in the morning, they'll look at you blankly and go, "Huh?" I am something of a morning person— heaven help the teens—and I tend to get out of bed, and gear up, and stuff gets done. So—according to the plan—I dropped off the kids at their schools and texted Jayce. "You ready to get things going, kiddo?"

Silence.

I gave it a few minutes. Twiddled my thumbs, sang nonsense songs in the car, whistled tunelessly (okay that one is a lie because I can't whistle) and I got more anxious as the minutes went by. Nothing. Nada.

Crap.

So I texted again, slightly more tersely.

"Yo. Jayce. What is the plan?"

More silence.

Now, I am generally a relatively rational person who can cope in a crisis, but I am not good at handling Not Knowing What The Hell Is Going On. In my (admittedly demented) mind I decided Jayce's parents had locked him in their basement dungeon (hey, I have a vivid imagination) and told him he was never ever getting out, complete with freakish Halloween-y muahuhuhahahaha laughter. All sorts of scenarios ran through my mind at light speed, each one more unsettling than the last, and so I sent one last text:

"Okay, I am headed up your way. Can you get back to me please?"

Still silence. Dammit.

I hit the road with no idea of where I actually needed to go and finally gave up on the texting thing and just called him. And got the teenager inarticulate noise of distress that meant, "Whyyyyyy are you waking me uuuuup? Go away." Rarely have I been that relieved to hear that sound of protest. Whew.

___

"Hey, Jayce, are you ready to get things rolling?"

Vague sputtering that meant yes… but how the heck were we going to go about this… but yes… but crap this was scary, but…

Circular thinking being unproductive I eventually put the kibosh on this discussion.

"Okay. Let's meet for breakfast."

He was able to respond to the offer of food in a somewhat focused way. Food has that effect. I fortified him with a bagel and myself with some coffee and we talked over logistics.

"I don't know how we are going to do this," he said, "My parents are NOT going to let you in their house."

"Well," said I, "I'm not leaving you alone with them for this, so what do we do?"

Eventually we hit on a plan that included me in the van at the curb a few houses down the street and him doing the packing. "I need to put my eyes on you every half hour or so," I told him. "Check in with me that often, please." He agreed, and we drove back to his parents' house and I parked the van, took a deep, shaky breath, and sent him on his way. I told him that if his parents wanted to meet me, they were welcome to come out and talk to me, and off he went.

A couple of minutes later his parents decided to take me up on my offer. They came down the street v-e-r-y s-l-o-w-l-y and I got out of the van and stood there awkwardly waiting for them to get to where I was.

"Good morning," I said, "I'm Kelly. Nice to meet you."

Jayce's dad made a foggy sort of greeting noise. His mother just stared at me. I stared back. Somebody had to speak up, so I did. "What would you like to know about me and my family?"

More staring.

"Well," I said into the echoing void, "I am married to a high school teacher, I have three girls (or so I believed at the time), I am sort of a normal suburban mom. I am a nurse and have been for a very long time. Jayce is renting out a room in our house and he will be safe and treated well there."

Again with the staring.

"No offense," said his dad, "but this whole thing seems very abrupt. We had a plan to allow Jayce to rent an apartment on his own." I was thoroughly annoyed by the mixture of new name and old gender he put out here in a misguided effort to be affirming.

"Yeah, sure you did," interjected Jayce, who had been standing by watching all the drama. "Now that you know this is really happening."

The conversation did not get less awkward, but it did get more amusing. "We know something about cults," said Jayce's dad. "We've seen people get indoctrinated into cults before and this looks a lot like that to us. We've been told things that are consistent with cult behavior."

Ohhh-kay.

My brain has a way of entertaining itself totally independently of my will, and so a bunch of thoughts flew through my skull about what sorts of refreshments might be available at meetings of the Transgender Cult. Like, would there always have to be cupcakes in trans flag colors? Would anything we served have to be fundamentally different on the inside than from the outside in an homage to transgender people? Clearly, I was going to need to do some more thinking about this problem, especially if I was expected to host these things. It also did not occur to me until much later to wonder when Jayce's parents had seen people indoctrinated into cults, and what the precise circumstances were.

A month or so later I somehow ended up in a very strange discussion with two other transgender friends. I recounted this insane story to them and asked what they thought the refreshments for cult meetings might be, and instantly and unanimously they agreed that the essential item was pickles. Why pickles I do not know, but pickles it had to be. When asked what kind of pickles, sweet, sour, garlic, dill, whatever, I got the response, "All the pickles." My friend Brianna says trans people like pickles. She says she learned it on Twitter.

I reflected for a minute on whether or not cult leaders usually drive beat up minivans with left wing bumper stickers plastered all over them.

"Um. No," I said. "I'm no cult leader, just an ordinary mom. We're planning to treat Jayce like the adult he is. He's completely free to come and go as he likes. I trust him to be able to make his own decisions."

"I don't," said his mom, "They're EXTREMELY immature and not at all ready to move out."

Now, "they" is a pronoun commonly chosen for use by people who classify themselves as nonbinary or agender. Jayce is unquestionably male and always has been. The correct pronouns for him are 'he, him, and his'. I get a tiny bit annoyed (okay, a lot) when people misgender trans kids by using the wrong pronouns. Basic etiquette says don't do that, and if you've ever met somebody who is trans and seen the effect this kind of misgendering has on them, you'll know how nasty it is. Their faces fall, they look lost and small, and then they visibly regroup and gather their strength again before they can move on. It's the equivalent of calling somebody an embarrassing name, except more fundamentally violent. It's a no-no.

While we're at it I need to throw out a digression about deadnaming. This is the act of referring to a transgender person using the name they were given at birth, which may have been carefully and lovingly chosen by doting parents who spent weeks poring over baby name books and trying out how various names sound when paired with phrases like 'Supreme Court Justice' or 'President' or 'Cardiothoracic Surgery Fellow'. Some parents do seem to name their children with absolute malice at the forefront of their brains, but in general, parents try to find a name that fits with their family names, traditions, ethnic or religious preferences, special meanings, or other cultural ideals. This fact is appreciated. The thing is, though, if you are a female to male transgender person and your original name is something generally considered feminine like, say, Celeste, you have a problem in a whole lot of places. School attendance, employment records, drivers' licenses, prescription bottles, and the name you are called in the eye doctor's waiting room will be positively crackling with the name Celeste when you know perfectly well that your real name, your *chosen* name, is Bob. Being called by a name that feels completely alien to your authentic identity hurts. Then you add in associations and experiences from your 'previous life', and you have the potential for awkwardness all over the place, and traumatic recall of events that occurred while you were living under that old name. Maybe you got bullied, belittled, or told you would never make it in your authentic gender role. Maybe you suffered abuse or exclusion, maybe your status wasn't accepted or authenticated by communities that you believed were connected to you and supportive of you. Many trans folks actively seek to prevent people from ever learning their deadnames, to the point of separating their lives before transition from their lives after transition.

For these reasons, a major pet peeve of mine is when people ask me or Jayce what his 'real' name is. His real name is Jayce. End of story. This is sometimes followed by, "Yes, but what is his 'correct' name?" and the answer is still, "Jayce," except this time it's pronounced in a slightly clipped tone of voice with a steely glare from me and a distinct chill in the air. Most people get the message at this point that shutting up might be in their best interest, but there's got to be one in every crowd who doesn't know when to quit banging on a question and who says something like, "Oh. Well, probably he just changed one letter or something, did I get it right?" Or they'll try pretending they're being circumspect and diplomatic in some other calculating manipulative way. There is quite literally no point in anyone reading this book asking us what his original name was. His ORIGINAL original name is lost in Russia someplace and is unlikely to be discovered even if somebody really goes crazy and tries to sleuth it out when he's famous for starring in this book. His pseudo-original (hey, I coined a word there) name is his own to keep, to use or not use, reveal or not reveal, as he sees fit. His REAL name is Jayce Kennedy Price, and he hears all three names when I feel the need to get parental with him. None of this should be difficult to understand.

I have found I can unnerve people completely by fixing them with a very direct stare and saying nothing whatsoever. Eventually people's eyes start to water a bit and they look away. Jayce just figures he should tell people his deadname is Princess Consuela Bananahammock, because he's nuts or because he's a *Friends* fan or both. I can get behind either reason.

That said, there is legal crap that has to be done in order to manage someone's bureaucracy, and the wheels of the system are greased with a sloppy mixture of arbitrary information about people that is collectively referred to as Identity. Someone's Identity includes name, other names, gender, a bunch of numbers like Social Security number and medical record numbers and such, and some bits of history like who declared them as a dependent on income tax and what addresses they lived at and whether or not they ever filed for bankruptcy or joined the Army or traveled to Bangladesh. The more of the grease of Identity that someone has, the easier it is to accomplish necessary bureaucratic tasks.

Back to the conversation with his parents that we left off on several pages ago before I started on my deadnaming rant. To recap, his mother has just informed me that 'they' are not mature enough to move out on 'their' own, thus pissing me off for one of the first times in our interactions with one another.

"Well," I said, "JAYCE is eighteen, and HE is capable of deciding that for HIMself. We are just offering him a safe space to live in." This was met with more of the staring and, "Did you think we were abusive? Because we're not abusive. I don't know what you were TOLD, but we're NOT ABUSIVE." I broke out my best de-escalation techniques and said that was good to know but Jayce was still planning to move out and so I would be right here waiting.

After this inspirational talk, Jayce went inside to start the packing process and his parents followed, presumably to supervise as their errant fledgling prepared to leave the nest, and I went on stakeout. This involved sitting in the van listening to terrible 80's music and eating whatever snacks came immediately to hand, including—but not limited to—leftover Teddy Grahams, half-fossilized fruit snacks, popcorn of questionable vintage, and someone else's Halloween candy. It also involved texting my friend Kari, who has a talent for talking me off ledges, usually by telling me to suck it the hell up because it will be okay.

"Kari. You would not believe the fun I am having here. You really would not." And she kept responding with useful stuff like, "Well, you don't see flames, so it must not be going too badly." Silver linings, people.

Twice during that first hour, Jayce came out to see me. About the time I would start to get really anxious (see: dungeon/evil laugh fantasy daydream above) he'd get in touch, a thing I was incredibly grateful for. He does have a talent for sending me one-word answers to questions, which drives me up the wall, but he did at least get back to me on a semi-routine basis. Plus, you know, no flames.

So I waited it out, singing along to AC/DC and Def Leppard in the car and screwing around on Facebook, and a little bit later it became evident that the coffee I'd consumed was a tactical error. I figured I'd need the caffeine, see, but that caffeine boost came with a largish cup of coffee, and so I was beginning to feel like you do when you're eight years old and on a road trip across some flyover state in your dad's beat-up Toyota station wagon with the 8-track playing and you see a sign that says, "Next rest stop 60 miles" and all of a sudden you kind of really need a stop. You KNOW your dad is going to say, "What do you mean you need a stop, you just peed 200 miles ago, we're never going to get there at this rate." Then he will do an exasperated huff and refocus his attention on Johnny Mathis on the 8-track and your battle of wills with your kidneys will begin.

"No, I'm good, I'll get through this," I thought to myself, trying not to think of brooks or rivers or any moving water whatsoever. Which of course completely failed to work. If you don't believe me, take five seconds right now and try not to think of a nine banded armadillo playing with a Koosh ball. The only way this would work for you is if you have no clue what either of those things are, and even then a part of your cognition will be devoting itself to the question, "What in hell is a nine banded armadillo and why would it play with something called a Koosh ball?"

"Fine, dammit," I thought, "I will hold out until the next half hour check in, I do not want to interrupt if good stuff is happening in there." And so I sat there again, trying not to think of Victoria Falls or the Pacific Ocean, and a few minutes later it became clear that the coffee had won and I was vanquished. "Jayce," I texted. "What do you think the odds are your parents would let me use their bathroom?"

"They say go to the Safeway," came the answer, because cult indoctrinators should never ever be allowed to use your bathroom or you might catch cult. It's a thing. I learned it on Twitter. I did a resigned sort of sigh with eye roll and thought what the hell, the Safeway was only a couple of blocks away and should therefore have been easy to find. "Okay," I texted back. "I'll be right back." I started the car, which for a wonder did not have a flat battery from having me sit in it running the stereo, and drove off in what I believed to be the direction of the Safeway. Which utterly eluded me. To this day I am convinced that the stupid Safeway store near the house Jayce grew up in somehow turned invisible or migrated to some other place or was just demolished and then rebuilt in the same day entirely so I wouldn't have a place to pee. Gas stations and Burger Kings and other assorted buildings with plumbing in them also did not seem to exist in that warped little corner of the world. It seemed downright sinister, a Machiavellian plot somehow orchestrated by Jayce's parents to ensure my downfall by causing my bladder to explode with a force that would fill the sky with body parts and yellow rain. I was pretty highly motivated not to get arrested that day as well, so finding a clump of bushes was also a nonviable option.

Then, mercifully, I spotted a Kaiser clinic. Sweet, blessed relief, combined with the hope that the bathroom I used hadn't previously contained somebody who was Patient Zero with some new and horrific pestilence that would wipe out my whole family. This is why there's hand sanitizer all over those places.

That business completed, I drove back to Jayce's parents' house and resumed my stakeout. An hour or so later I got a miraculous message from Jayce: "I think we're about ready."

"Okay cool," I said, and pulled the van forward to the driveway, figuring that loading the accumulated worldly possessions of a child of eighteen years might take a little time.

Nope. Two boxes. Not even big boxes. Each of my kids could fill up eight or nine boxes just with books before they ever started on the old artwork, food wrappers, McDonald's toys, mismatched doll clothes, and single socks that seem to constitute most of their worldly wealth. "I think we can get your bike, if you want it," I said to him, "And also your helmet, because you gotta wear a helmet."

"They have a new helmet," said his mother, "But they'll never wear it."

"I'll wear it," said Jayce.

Possessions he was allowed to take included all of his clothes that were designed for a boy, school stuff and recording equipment he had purchased for himself, a guitar and backpack, and that was about all. He was not allowed to take his own mattress or bedroom furniture or any keepsakes or collectibles. I asked if he wanted to say goodbye to his parents and he said no, he'd say 'see you soon' instead, and his mother called him by the correct name for what he later told me was the very first time.

In a slight state of combat fatigue, we left and drove back to the Price house. I had gotten the office mostly cleared out except for a couple of bookshelves and the computer desk, which is not a desk at all but rather a very battered old table that I've had forever and that holds a lot of stuff. We took the computer apart and relocated it to our bedroom, then took the table apart, and then Jayce and I attempted to move the damn table up the stairs.

It turns out neither of us is physically equipped for moving large items in any direction that involves an upward path. Oh, the table legs were easy. Hell, I could even carry two of those at a time. I was feeling kinda badass about that, and so we got the table top to the bottom of the stairs and looked up at the Kilimanjaro that is the main staircase at Casa Price. The top was shrouded in clouds and we could hear the distant calls of soaring birds of prey lost somewhere in the dizzying heights.

"Have we got this, Jayce?" I asked, and was assured that yes, barring avalanches, we could handle it, and so we hefted the tabletop and started up, suppressing the urge to yodel and thinking of goats and whether or not we should have hired sherpas.

Now, my stairs do not go up in one straight flight. Instead there are two landings and you go up a few steps and then turn left, and then you go up a few more and turn left again, and then you go up the last few and you're at the top. This configuration has advantages and disadvantages. The advantages are that you do have an opportunity to stop and rest on your way up, maybe break out the binoculars and look back toward the tiny Lego village of Kathmandu on the plain far below. On the way DOWN you can only fall so far and are therefore theoretically less likely to actually break bones and more likely to have your family give you a slow clap and say, "Way to go, Grace." Disadvantages, however, include the fact that there is no way to move something heavy and rigid from bottom to top without going around a couple of corners.

So we got to about the fourth step up and this was when Jayce looked at the landing and, channeling Ross Geller from *Friends* in the episode where they try to haul a sofa upstairs, said "Pivot!" and I immediately caught the cultural reference by some weird telepathy and was off in gales of unhinged moonbat giggling. Some of this hysteria was caused by stress, of course, and some by my own tendency to find things hilarious that cause other people to look at me like maybe I should lay off the nitrous for a while, but the contagion got Jayce, too, and in three seconds flat we were both laughing so hard we nearly dropped the damn table.

Of course, just about the time we were beginning to get a grip it then fell to me to pick up Chandler Bing's part and say, "Shut up!" and we were off again. Then after manhandling the table up to the next landing one of us said something about how we really need to work out, creating another paroxysm of hilarity, and then somehow we gained the top at last.

"Dude," I asked after we'd put the table to rights and gone back downstairs, "you have two boxes and school stuff. What the hell took so long getting you packed up this morning?"

"Ohhhh…" he answered, "my mom made me go through all the girl clothes and tell her what I didn't want. Which was everything." Then he stood and looked thoughtful for a minute and said, "Any chance of getting me back to Boulder today? I have to go to work."

"Wow." I said, "You don't think today you might be justified in calling in sick?" I had to go pick up all the younger kids and there wasn't going to be time or opportunity to get him back there before his shift started.

He shook his head decisively. "No, it will be busy, my boss needs me. I'll take an Uber."

Jayce: Pivot!

Moving Day was not only the craziest day of my life, it was also the most terrifying. I was preparing to pack everything up and figure out what I was going to take. I still thought I had a week left. I was trying to say goodbye to my childhood home, my neighborhood, and everything that I was leaving behind. Nothing prepares you for this at all.

The second I broke the news to my parents, life just got harder. There wasn't a second that I wasn't getting screamed at. I wanted to pack my clothes, my Legos, my recording equipment, my favorite movies, and other irreplaceable items, many of which I did not get to take. I wasn't even allowed to take my mattress, or anything else that they had bought, because they said since I was leaving, nothing was mine any longer.

I got home from work and I had gotten some boxes that Kelly's friend Michelle had lent to me. She wanted them back but she never did get them because my dad decided he needed them for something. It's funny, because at the time I asked if I would ever meet this woman who loaned me the boxes, and the answer was yes but that's a story for another time.

Anyhow, I was trying my best to get everything together, but between all the arguing and screaming it was unbelievably hard. I suppose it was good that I was kept busy, because that meant I didn't have time to think about how sad and scared I was. I couldn't believe I was really doing this. I never thought I would have the courage to actually walk out the door. The last night was chaotic, and also dangerous, and so I texted Kelly that I was fine for one more night.

Apparently, the "one more night" part registered on Kelly's radar as concerning, because as things turned out we ended up moving me out the next day.

Remember that week I thought I had to get ready for this transition? Whoops.

I met Kelly for breakfast after telling my parents "Well, I'm leaving in a few hours." My mom said "Wait, today?"

"Yup."

Now my former mother couldn't really do anything to stop me because Kelly was already outside in the van, and she knew it. After breakfast we began the final packing. This took longer than I expected, because my mother decided that after a year of me telling her I was a boy, and living as a boy and wearing boys' clothing, she thought this was the perfect time to go through all my *girl* clothes and try and convince me to take them.

"I think you should take your bras; you might need them!" She actually said this. And I said, "Why would I need them, I've been binding for over a year, happily living as a male, so why the hell does THIS make any sense?"

Oh. That's right. It doesn't.

After that fun morning, we were finally ready to start loading, and since I was still trying to maintain some kind of relationship with my parents, I thought it would be right to introduce them to Kelly and at least tell them where I was going.

This turned out to be like sailing on jagged rocks (weird metaphor) because it didn't go well. My mother just stared, and my father shocked us all by telling Kelly that her family's offer looked a lot like I was being indoctrinated into a cult. I was trying really hard not to laugh, but with all the insanity going on at that moment I forgot to ask him what the story was there. What was his experience with cults?

Anyhow, that meeting did not go well, and back in the house I got called all sorts of dehumanizing things, but once we announced that we were ready to go, my mother called me Jayce for the very first time. She had called me a lot of other names, but never Jayce. She hugged me and said, "I love you," and this was incredibly confusing because I knew it was manipulation, but it was also something I had wanted to hear her say forever. I knew she was hoping that I'd say, "Never mind," unpack everything, and remain her little puppet forever. But I didn't. And I will *never* forget telling my father "I'm not saying goodbye. I'm saying, 'see you later.'" From my mother all I got as I left was a death glare, a cold shoulder, and a slammed door.

As we left, I didn't look back. I couldn't believe what I had just done. The whole ride to my new home, I was in shock and couldn't believe this was real.

We arrived home and I was greeted by our dog, a goofy terrier named Callie. I've never been a huge dog person but I said, "hey if I have to have a dog, I'm glad she's little." I got introduced to the cats too, which was good because I love cats. Nobody else was home, it was just Kelly and I.

After I greeted the animals, our next task was to make the office into a semi-livable space for the night. Currently, the office has been transformed into my bedroom and I got to set it up how I wanted and that was a privilege I had never gotten before. My former room was so girly, and everything, literally everything was various shades of pink. I hated it, I refused to sleep in there for eight months, but I was never allowed to change it.

We had to move Daniel's computer and table up the stairs to the bedroom, and this is when I discovered two things. One, Kelly and I obviously both needed to start working out, and secondly, I had just found the world's best mother; the best fit for me. We often say that we share the same brain and the same sense of humor. My first glimpse of this was when we were trying to haul the damn table up the stairs and I channeled *Friends* character Ross Geller and yelled "Pivot!" I was really hoping Kelly would fill Chandler's part and yell "Shut up!" And she did. Nothing made me happier and it's those stupid little moments that began on day one that now make our mother-son relationship what it is. We bonded very quickly and that silly little exchange was the start of it.

Chapter 5

Kelly: Dysphoria, Hygiene, and You

I mentioned that I'm a nurse, right? When most people think of nurses they have a tendency to envision one of three scenarios. These are: brisk middle-aged women in starched pinafores, Julianna Margulies telling Dr. Mark Green where he could stick some inane misdiagnosis he was about to make in the ER, or bad porn. Now those of you who know me in person will be completely unable to picture me as a ministering angel of mercy in any of these roles. I can be brisk if you piss me off, but starched anything is a hell no and I don't know what a pinafore even is, exactly. I have occasionally told a doctor to quit being a moron and engage in decisive medical action (for which I will get no credit.) And any porn I am likely to get involved in will be GOOD porn.

The first weekend Jayce lived with us, I was gone the whole weekend. By the time I arrived home from my weekend camp nursing job, I was a zombie with some fun stories to tell, and I admit I didn't spend a hell of a lot of time thinking about how life was going at Casa Price. Sunday afternoon I escaped—I mean clocked out—and went home. It kind of appeared as though a cyclone had hit the house, but that was business as usual, and nobody seemed the worse for wear, so we passed an agreeable enough evening and the next day was Monday.

Remember the thing I told you about what happens when you wake teenagers up in the morning? Well, here is another fact about life with the creatures: If they are allowed to stew in their own juices there will be chemical reactions created that result in a cloud of teenager stench that requires hazmat assistance to resolve. More than once I have had the job of carpool driver for a gang of Kaiden's friends, and each addition to the population of the car has resulted in a visible thickening of the atmosphere inside that is simply not alleviated by the countering effects of little cardboard air-fresheners shaped like trees. Lest you think this is something that applies only to boys, I am here to disabuse you of the notion, because teens of all genders are capable of creating a deadly miasma of unbelievable proportions. Monday night, therefore, I stated firmly that all children over the age of five were showering. No, I mean it. Get ye in there, kids, after playing rock-paper-scissors to see who goes first, and while you're at it do something with the dirty laundry. This seemed to me to be a typical conversation of the type that occurs thousands of times a day in homes all over the nation. Kaiden is a typical teen in this respect in that he's got stuff he'd rather do than preen in front of a mirror, and so we've always had to kind of prod him into the bathroom and into the shower. I'm not prone to Mom Guilt, nor to any kind of angst over whether or not my little snowflakes are feeling validated and motivated at all times. This particular night we had an issue, though, and I am still apologizing to Jayce for it.

One of the clinical aspects of being transgender is a lovely little thing called dysphoria. This word has an elegant sound, like the name of a Jane Austen heroine or a Victorian era noblewoman, but you may rest assured the condition it describes is anything but pretty. The dictionary defines it as, *'a profound feeling of unease or dissatisfaction'.* There are a variety of different types of dysphoria, several of which apply to a body-brain disconnection in which a person's identity does not match their body appearance or type. People with the condition literally feel as if they are living in the wrong body. They have a belief that some aspect of their body is incredibly flawed and that this needs to be dealt with by almost any method necessary in order to function. It causes serious anxiety and can lead to depression and even suicide if it gets bad enough. Jayce's particular variant of this is known as gender dysphoria, and it is debilitating.

Now, think about how you handle a shower, assuming you do not have dysphoria. Maybe you crank up some tunes and sing along, hopefully you use soap and shampoo and clean, hot water. Probably you strip off and walk to the shower past a mirror in your bathroom without a second thought, and your mind wanders sort of peacefully as you stand in your cloud of fragrant steam. Once your ablutions are complete, you step out, towel off, and start screwing around with the things you do to make yourself look and feel more like YOU. Hairstyling, skin care, maybe makeup if you're going out, whatever. Eventually most of us take a last look in the mirror and leave the bathroom and get on with other aspects of life.

This is not the case for somebody with gender dysphoria. A glance at themselves in the mirror can trigger all different types of emotional pain. Having to wash themselves theoretically involves having to touch their own bodies in intimate (and hopefully cleansing) ways. They're absolutely exhausted after a shower, which should be a pleasant soothing sort of experience. Some kids with gender dysphoria are distressed to the point of incontinence because they perceive the body they live in as, "not me." So, Jayce went and took his shower, and then Kaiden went and took his, and later that night he came to me and said, "Mom. We can't do that again." I, of course, had no clue what he was talking about, but he can be rather sophisticated, and so he did an eyeroll at me and said, "Mom. Dysphoria." The light dawned at last and I thought, holy crap, Price, you've had the responsibility for caring for this kid for less than a week and already you managed to force him into exacerbating his mental distress. Way to go.

So the next day I cornered him alone and said, "Jayce. We need to talk. I owe you an apology for last night, and we need to try to figure some stuff out." He looked at me like I'd grown a third eye and went, "Huh?" and I said that I hadn't even thought about the dysphoria triggering effects of a normal shower and that we could figure out some ways to deal with it to make it easier.

That conversation kind of blew his mind. "Wow," he said, "I hate it. I always have, but I'll try." Meanwhile my brain was ticking over and trying to come up with concrete, painless things we could do to make the process easier for Jayce and get me out of the cloud of teenage funk wafting above my house. Here is Price's First Actual Piece Of Guidance. What are we now, five chapters in? Better late than never, I give you;

The Transgender Teen Boy:

The Shower Plan

Cover up the mirror. If you're feeling ambitious or you have multiple people using the same bathroom who might need the mirror you could make a little curtain that draws to close over it, kind of like the one in Sirius Black's house they use to stop the portrait of his mother from screaming at everyone. If you're feeling cheap and you just need a quick solution you stick a garbage bag (opaque and black, naturally) over it and slap some painters' tape you find in the garage on it. In our house, Kaiden and Jayce are the ones who use that particular bathroom and it's totally painless to just leave the trash bag over it because neither of them cares about the mirror. Plus, it will act as a nice accent if we ever decide to sell the place, so I think we'll just leave it up.

Darkness Is Your Friend. Really, this one seemed totally logical once I thought about it a little bit. I mean how often have you heard women complaining about terrible lighting in bathrooms and how it seems to throw all their perceived body flaws into sharp relief? We look in the mirror and go, "This lighting is so harsh, it really brings out my [stretch marks, extra nose, whatever]. A kid with dysphoria goes, "This lighting is so harsh, it really brings out my AAAAAAAAAAHHHH! What is that? That's not me! HELP!" If there's a room in the house that should always have dimmer switches installed in it, the bathroom really is that room. I suppose this is another case of 'if you're feeling ambitious', because you could install dimmer switches in there, but here we have gone for the highly economical 'just leave the light off and shower after sunset' method.

But Not Total Darkness. You really do need a little light in there. Not much, but bathrooms are notoriously slippery, hazardous places anyway, so not falling headfirst into the toilet seems like a good goal. If you're going for a soap opera ambience thing you could do something like a candle or two, and the aforementioned dimmer switches could come in handy, but we have settled for setting a headlamp with a red LED light on the counter. After Jayce gets all clean and shiny he's therefore equipped to go spelunking, should he be so inclined. I figure you never know, best to be prepared. Some day he might come out of there with the headlamp on and ask for a bag of sandwiches to take into a cave someplace. Also we are avoiding candles because we have cats and small children and house fires are not in the plan, and scented candles are girly anyhow.

The Axe Thing. Okay I am not a big fan of cologne or perfume or any such thing for guys, I think they generally smell weird wearing those things. Smelling like you've been dipped in bug killer and allowed to dry over a low flame is not attractive

63

in my book. However, if you look around the grocery store you are going to find that most of the soaps and body wash products available are marketed to the tastes of women, because we tend to do the shopping for our families. Even Ivory Soap has a clean sort of floral smell. If you're a teen trans boy with gender dysphoria, this is not going to work. You really, really need something that smells clean, but in a masculine way, and preferably something that lasts awhile so you don't have Price bitching about teen boy stench anymore, because that gets old. Enter Axe. I don't know what they put in this stuff but they've got this really easy line of products that are pretty much guaranteed to have some scent that evokes woods at night and a successful hunt for buffalo rather than fields of violets and tea roses. I like this cedar/sandalwood thing they have because it's a shampoo AND a body wash so two birds with one stone and all that.

Assorted Equipment. Use of: This requires a whole chapter pretty much all to itself, but I will just put this out here. Trans guys do some stuff on a daily basis to manage their dysphoria. Some people use tape or a binder to decrease chest dysphoria, others use a packer (which is a sort of prosthetic penis) to decrease genital dysphoria, and wearing any or all of these devices in the shower is way, way better than not showering at all. One caveat is that a wet binder that is really tight might require the intervention of a rescue team with the Jaws of Life to get out of after a shower, so using one that's old and worn out or slightly too large is a better plan if you don't have a firefighter in your family. Or, they can just shower in a swimsuit. It ain't that big a deal.

Dude Wipes and Similar. Yes, this is a thing. These are basically like oversized baby wipes for personal cleaning and/or the kind of wipes used for convalescence for bed baths. They generally come pre-impregnated with soap or skin cleanser, and some of them you can even warm up. You can order them online or pick them up at a medical supply store. That way if the dysphoria is really bad your kid has another option for staying clean.

Really the key is to just make sure you've talked things out and put a plan in place so your child feels supported and try new things if the first thing you try doesn't work. You have to be very candid and very flexible in your thinking, but clean teens are definitely worth a little extra effort and thought.

Jayce: Smells like Axe

This chapter focuses on an incident that I actually consider astonishing when I look back on it, because prior to this it had never occurred to me that there are ways to cope with dysphoria that are easy and concrete. Before I got to the point where I could be treated with hormone replacement therapy (weekly testosterone injections) and top surgery (removal of breast tissue), there were more immediate issues to be addressed. I have lived with gender dysphoria throughout my life but there were some things I just thought I had to tolerate.

The first weekend I was at the Prices' house I didn't shower at all. Kelly came home from her weekend camp nursing job on Sunday and practically made it her life's mission to throw me in the shower. I didn't blame her, so I just said okay, didn't think twice and suffered through it like I always had. Then Kaiden, who is also trans, caught something that we didn't. He went to see Kelly and said "Mom! Pay attention! Showering causes Jayce dysphoria, can't you see that?"

Showering in the wrong body is painful because all you can think about is how everything feels wrong. I have sometimes described gender dysphoria as a feeling like there are cockroaches crawling over my skin, and showering used to make it a lot worse. After my shower Kelly approached me to apologize. Like I said, I now find this funny because it didn't occur to me what the heck she was apologizing for! Nobody in my life previously ever cared that I was in the wrong body, so why now? I figured getting clean was another daily opportunity to disassociate and just get it over with. When Kelly was actually concerned with helping me, I was nothing short of shocked. I made it clear that I had always hated showers but what could we do about that? I didn't want to make extra work for anyone because I felt like I had already created enough work.

It turns out there are things that can be done. Darkness is beautiful but you still don't want to slip across the floor when you get out of the shower so headlamps can be useful. If you have to, wear swim shorts or a loose binder. You'll get cleaner than you were before. Also, no need to be classy, just take a black trash bag and cover the mirror. That way, you won't spend too much time thinking about everything you can't stand about your body. Once I was made aware of these things, the difference was like night and day. I felt much better about showers and still couldn't believe anyone cared that much. All of these were very useful interventions for many months, and they could be helpful ideas for trans kids everywhere. I know I'm not the only one that had no idea that treating shower dysphoria was even an option.

Chapter 6

Kelly: Too Sexy For These Girl Clothes

Most of us do not think of a shopping trip to buy clothes for a boy as anything but an errand, at least unless the kid in question is getting married or something that requires a mom to look at him in a rented tuxedo and go, "Aww, my little man is all grown up!" and then wipe a lone tear from her eye. Jayce, however, came to us in kind of dire straits as far as apparel went. I gather from him that he had a lot of girl clothes that he of course flatly refused to wear, and that the issue of sartorial splendor for a teen guy was one that really had not been addressed. Not to mention the fact that I knew little to nothing about how to shop for a boy. I was about as clueless as it is possible to be other than to mentally catalog my knowledge of how boys dress and have the phrase 'dinosaurs and bulldozers' float through my brain in a disconnected sort of way. Young men in their late teens do not generally wear a lot of dinosaurs and bulldozers, it turns out.

———

Dinosaurs and bulldozers are more a theme among the 4–6-year-old set, along with graphic tees that say things like *Mommy's Little Monster* on them. It also turned out that despite the amazing number of boys of all ages I am acquainted with, I apparently never look closely at any of them, because I had no idea.

Cosmic timing being what it is, I had been in possession of a 30% off coupon at Kohl's that had expired a couple of days before Jayce needed a major shopping trip. Oh well.

Anyway, we set off on a Friday morning. This is a theme; Friday mornings have been reserved for Getting A Bunch Of Shit Done and/or Driving All Over Hell. We hit the boys' department like a runaway train. Jayce took a sort of bewildered look around and said, "What's my budget?" and I said, "Well, what do you need?" and he looked around and said, "Pretty much everything, I think."

"Dude," I said, "I'm gonna go get a cart."

It actually turned out that we were halfway synchronized in the things we thought would look good on him. I am not a half bad personal shopper for my kids, because they're generally relatively non-discerning in the fashion department. Kaiden will wear any tee with an 80's metal band logo on it, Gabi will wear any dress or anything with Minecraft on it, and Mari is into basketball shorts and Pikachu. Everyone gets tie-dyes because Daniel's classes do that every year as a science project and I get the leftover dye, so it always looks like we've been transformed into Haight-Ashbury in the summertime. All we need is love beads and Nehru jackets to make the whole look complete, and a Toyota Sienna minivan is not that far from a VW Microbus in terms of style and function, although it is exponentially less cool.

Anyway, apparently I did relatively well because I'd hold something up and Jayce would go, "Cool" and stick one of every color of whatever it was in the cart. We even found him a swimsuit at 80% off. He didn't end up with a single dinosaur or bulldozer, either. We wandered through the store and gathered things together and then he hit the dressing room and tried everything on, which took like 45 minutes, because there was a LOT of stuff. Then after he accomplished all that he tried to get it all to fit back in the cart to no avail. "I have never been allowed to do this," he said, "I have never been allowed to just pick my own clothes." I got my mind blown a little bit by how this simple errand that is totally taken for granted by millions of moms all across the country could be greeted with wide-eyed wonder by a kid who'd had to fight every day of his life to just be himself. And then it was time to buy underwear.

"What kind of underwear do you like?" I asked as we perused the options in that part of the store.

He stopped and stared at me, dumbstruck. "I have absolutely no idea!" he said, and this struck both of us as uproariously funny at the same time – again – and we stood together in the men's underwear section at Kohl's and laughed until we couldn't breathe and probably gave the security people whose job it is to watch the security videos a lot to wonder about. We had to lean on each other and wheeze for a while before we could even walk.

We headed for the checkout, still giggling psychotically, and on the way things in the cart kept sort of slithering off the top of the pile and onto the floor. We could go about five feet before something else would fall off. These clothes were trying to escape, I am convinced of it.

Once we got there it was time to let the poor, beleaguered cashier wonder what on earth was wrong with us. You could see this poor lady thinking, "Oh God, why the hell couldn't I be on break right now?" We picked up everything that had slid to the floor—again—and started piling things on the counter to be checked out. The cashier looked at me sort of doubtfully and asked if we wanted to keep the hangers. I thought briefly about what I knew of teenagers and said, "Jayce, what are the odds you'll ever actually hang up clothes?" and he said, "Probably pretty damn low, if I'm being honest!" and you guessed it; cue more stupid laughter. The cashier started putting everything into a plastic bag that could conceivably have doubled as the Goodyear blimp in a pinch. I went to lift this monstrosity off the counter and it just about yanked my arm out of the socket. Jayce thought I was just being goofy, because that was the pattern of the day, and so I mustered up the energy to lift the thing up straight-armed with three fingers and said, "Fine, you carry it". He reached out and grabbed it and I let go, and, FWOMP! it yanked him to the floor, which was of course grounds for more hysteria. We did get out of there at last, but I am relatively certain that the extra weight in the back lifted the front tires of my van completely off the ground. Traction control is a beautiful thing.

That was the most fun I have ever had on a shopping trip in my life, and it was one of those things you do that you will remember forever. You know how occasionally you get a good day, one that creates a memory that you'll unpack occasionally over the coming years and look at and enjoy again? That day is one of those for me.

Clothes may make the man, but new glasses and a decent haircut (okay, Great Clips. I have four kids, sue me for not blowing forty bucks on one haircut) also help dramatically. This would be one of those times where my friends have stepped up and rocked the house once again. I mentioned I have friends that are so totally fabulous that they are worth their weight in any precious substance you can name, remember? Well, every time I would photograph Jayce in the early days, he'd yank off his glasses and stare sort of blearily in what he hoped was the direction of the camera. It looked as though I was harboring somebody who was either moderately drunk or who was trying to interpret airport signs in a foreign language while running late to catch a flight at 4:00 in the morning. I kept thinking of Velma from *Scooby Doo* going, "My glasses! I can't see without them!" and accidentally putting her hand down on the hairy appendage of whatever 70's-era cartoon monster the gang were debunking in any given episode. It was clear that nothing was. Clear, that is. But as we have established, I have apparently not spent all that much time actually looking at teenaged boys, because although *I* didn't see anything wrong with his glasses, HE clearly DID. Eventually we had an explanatory conversation that went, "Jayce, why in hell do you yank your glasses off every time I take your picture?" followed by, "Because I hate them, they're girly," and Price had another one of her epiphanies of 'duh' and called to schedule the kid an eye exam.

Now, the Kohl's bill from the previous couple of pages was kinda... well... massive. And I had a bunch of people familiar with my situation ("Holy shit, we have another kid, I got him at Noodles & Company!") who kept asking me what size clothes Jayce wears. I did not want to seem ungrateful, truly I did not, but this kid had never really been allowed to choose anything for himself and so I declined their kind offers and said, "But he does need a new pair of glasses...." knowing that it was somewhat unlikely that people were going to expect him to wear the hand me down glasses their kid had two years ago.

Well, two mamas, Paula Langhorst and Elizabeth Panzer, stepped up and kicked in some cash, and my sweet Kaiden, who considers himself Jayce's sibling and who will take on anyone who says otherwise with his teeth, kicked in some more. We pulled the rest together and Jayce was able to select some very masculine frames, and while we were at it the eye doctor looked him over and said, "Whoa, dude, your eyes have changed!" and so he got the whole works taken care of. Now I spend some time each day plaguing him to actually clean the glasses, because I swear he lives in a perpetual fog, but at least he's happy enough with them to leave them on for photos and therefore he appears much more focused. This is good news, because he takes a whole lot of selfies. I of course give him all manner of crap about this, and one day recently I said, "Dude, with all those selfies in there you're not gonna have any room for pics of Emma Watson," and he said, "32 gigs," which sent me completely around the bend. I'm pretty sure now that if he ever sends any of his selfies to Emma Watson she won't assume he's drunk, and she WILL say, "wow, who is that dude with the cool glasses who sent me this? I really must meet him, ASAP." Well maybe not, but a boy can dream.

Jayce: Glasses and Hair Also Need Work

When I look back at the first year of this whole crazy experience, my first clothes shopping trip to Kohl's with my mom always stands out for a couple of reasons. For one, we could not stop laughing, and most of the time we forgot what we were laughing about. Secondly, this was a completely new experience, which is part of what made it so entertaining.

Before I moved in, I lived my whole life never feeling comfortable in my own clothes. I didn't even really have a say about what I got to wear. As a young child, my mother picked out all of my clothes, and I wasn't allowed to leave the house unless she approved of what I had on. By the way, these were never clothes fit for a boy. Of course not. It was all pink, glitter, fake fur, or skin tight. None of this ever felt like it was made for me.

During one illustrating event from my teen years, I recall being fifteen at the time, and I was absolutely screaming about wearing a dress to a formal neighborhood gathering. I was practically crying because I just felt so uncomfortable, and there was no way all of this pre-approved fashion crap looked right on me. One of the other guests asked my mother, "Why don't you just let them go home and change? They are clearly miserable".

She finally gave in. It was no easy task, but the second I was able to throw on black pants and a solid gray shirt, I was a different person. I'm convinced that I spent the majority of my early life dressing like a terrible drag queen. If I ever got lucky enough to pick out my school clothes without my mother, I went straight for ripped jeans, basketball shorts, jerseys, or solid color t-shirts. The first day I ever got to wear something like this in public was in 6th grade, and nothing ever felt better.

With all of this in mind, when I got to go to Kohl's with Kelly, I was blown away that I had the freedom to choose things I actually wanted to wear. Honestly, I'm not too picky. If I like it, I'll buy it in five colors. I used to DESPISE Kohl's absolutely and would do anything to get out of going. Bra shopping was torture. Shopping with my mother seemed like it was cruel and unusual punishment. However, on that day with Kelly, I was thinking of two things. One, I can't believe this is real, and I'm allowed to dress like a boy because I am a boy! Yay! Secondly, I hope Kelly doesn't turn around and hand me the bill. I'll make up for it in chores. Maybe.

It's like a whole new world was opened that day because I was accepted, encouraged to be comfortable, and even had fun. It no longer felt like a chore or a reason for screaming all day, like it did with my former mother. Now, all Kelly and I could do was make our way through the store and laugh like idiots. I had never gotten to choose my socks, let alone underwear, so when she asked me what my preference was, we both lost it, hysterically laughing because I had no idea! Before now, I never knew shopping could be fun.

When it came time to check out, we still didn't stop laughing. I feel sorry for the poor lady who checked us out. I think she quit that day. I don't blame her. She asked me about hangers, and I was pretending to think about it for a moment, but I knew that there was no chance I would hang anything up. This caused more hysterical laughter. Since that was the pattern for the day, when Kelly grabbed the bag of clothes and it dropped to the floor with a THUD, I figured she was kidding. Then I found out for myself. Nope. Heavy as hell. We left, and shopping without screaming or crying was a milestone for me. Every moment like this with Kelly was just another glimpse into what my life was turning into, and the reality of the situation kept sinking in with one positive experience after another.

Chapter 7

Kelly: Tupperware and Tears

If you've read this far you hopefully have done some thinking and some laughing, which are, as I said way back in the intro, part of the point of the book. By now, though, people have to be wondering if this whole transition came with literally no emotional upheaval whatsoever, and since answering that question with, "Nope" makes for uninteresting reading, I will tell you about that part.

This brings me to a point of contention between Jayce and myself. When all is well, Mama Bear Price over here can usually count on some semi-regular text messages from Jayce of the 'What's for dinner?' variety. Occasionally he'll throw out something a tiny bit more descriptive and energetic, but when he's busy or stressed he'll send me back these single word responses to questions that are both incomplete AND exasperating. "How are you doing?" will be met with, "OK". "Do you need anything at the grocery store?" yields, "Yes", with no actual indication of what items might be required, and so I just hazard guesses and hope for the best.

Once in a while, though, something will occur that is genuinely worrying for me given that I adore this kid and want nothing more than for him to be a safe, happy, healthy boy and to get to meet Emma Watson. Sometimes this is a conversation with his parents. Sometimes it is a conversation with his own brain in which his trauma tells him lies about things and leads him to believe that up is down and that his life before he got here was perfectly normal and he is a Bad Kid for putting his parents through hell because the shit that happened to him was all his own fault. Other times the precipitating event is just something that happened at work or an old friend behaving in a new and disturbing way.

Compounding this is the fact that Jayce finds it completely intolerable to be the cause of someone else's pain. Most of the time he'll literally compromise himself and his own life and safety in order to avoid it. I admit that to me this is terrifying because when he's in that emotional state he is dangerously vulnerable and very much at risk, but fortunately the kid has a core of steel and someplace way inside of all the grief there's a little guiding spirit that only allows him to put up with so much and then no more. He is slowly learning to listen to his own heart and to identify his own truths and it has gotten harder for him to be gaslighted and manipulated the way he used to be—a thing I am profoundly grateful for.

Coping with the 'ouch' moments (and hours and days) has required the use of some concrete strategies for all of us. For

Jayce, his previously favorite way of dealing with this stuff was to dissociate himself completely from it and wait for it to catch up with him later on at a time he perceived to be more convenient for a breakdown, and then shake himself to pieces all alone. He will literally fight it off all day long, visibly holding himself together and gradually growing wilder and more manic until finally—wham! Ignition. One of us stays with him when he gets that way. Sometimes he'll calm down and pull himself back out of it, other times he gets to cope with what we have decided to call *Jaycequakes*.

Crying, apparently, is a sign of weakness, especially if you are a guy, and it is also something of a dysphoria trigger if you see it that way. The fact is that crying can be good for you because it's cathartic and helps you clear stress hormones from your body without ending up with the cellular damage and inflammation caused by the buildup of cortisol. This means you age well and stay healthier, gain less in visceral fat as you get older, and recover faster from episodes that are emotionally intense. It's a skill that increases resiliency. People who cry look better when they go to their high school reunions years down the line. That is my story and I am sticking to it.

It's also, not to put too fine a point on it, kind of damp. Your face goes red and blotchy and your eyes get bloodshot and there are boogers involved. Crying on someone's shoulder literally means crying ON someone's shoulder. I have often conjectured about exactly what evolutionary advantage could possibly be conferred by having body fluids leak out of your face when you're emotional. Crying requires a lot of energy and a lot of resources, and evolution doesn't really support traits that don't result in more offspring left behind, so there must be SOME reason for it. I also used to wonder why pregnancy—for me, anyway—comes with apocalyptic nausea and the consumption of gallons of candied jalapeno peppers instead of, say, a little patch of skin on your body someplace that turns blue or something so you know to start nesting. Anyhow, there must be something about a good cry that increases fertility or makes you more likely to be supported or something that facilitates the production and raising of the next generation. I welcome input on this from any researcher-types who read this book and have ideas.

Jayce is not much of a crier. Instead of crying he is seized with the shakes and will quite literally vibrate the entire floor in a way that registers on seismographs miles away, hence the name '*Jaycequakes*'. These things have to be very good for burning calories, it's sort of like sitting next to a very large hummingbird in full flight. Sometimes he'll shake for a few minutes and the storm will pass. Other times the episode progresses into a full-blown panic attack during which he isn't really present and doesn't really know what's happening, he just knows he's terrified. We stay with him when these things happen, holding onto him when he needs us. He's not allowed to be alone with those feelings because he's at risk for hurting himself and he tends to dissociate, and because sucky feelings should really be shared with somebody supportive who cares about you. He generally recovers faster and feels better in the aftermath if he has somebody who loves him close by to ride it out with him. Kaiden has a special talent in this respect, he can sit there in a state of perfect calm and keep telling Jayce that it will pass and he's not going anywhere and to just let it take the wheel until it's over because we will keep him safe. Jayce will growl out some desire that Kaiden go away and leave him alone with it and he just says, "Nope" in a relaxed sort of voice and keeps doing his sibling thing.

Panic attacks in most cases are self-limiting because after 20-30 minutes the body's biochemical engines that make epinephrine start to run out of fuel. Note; epinephrine used to be called adrenaline, and a little bit of it when you're being chased by a bear is a good thing but a lot of it when you're sitting in your living room at night is less productive. If you're able to just sit with those scary, racing feelings and let them have their way with you, it gets better and goes away. People in the midst of an attack often feel like they are going to die, have a heart attack, go crazy (whatever that means) or some similar thing, but really these attacks aren't dangerous in and of themselves. It's a big deal if someone with panic attacks is aware of this fact because the underlying terror can be tempered by a slightly cooler, 'This sucks, but it won't kill me' thought. Jayce also likes to tell me that I didn't sign up for this shit and I should really just go to bed, and I just say oh yes, I did, I knew exactly what I was getting into when you moved in and it's all good.

If you've been paying attention you may have noted that the title of this chapter is *Tupperware and Tears*. You are now thinking, okay, the tears I get, but what in hell does Tupperware have to do with anything? Well, let us clarify this for you now.

The three major emotional states that, for Jayce, feel terrible and debilitating and traumatic are fear, sadness, and anger. Fear and sadness we've kind of covered, but anger is the reason for the Tupperware.

Maybe you are familiar with the concept of a Rage Room. This is a place where things exist that are meant for people to just beat hell out of until they feel better. Picture a big warehouse-type space with soundproofing where you can scream like a banshee and smash ceramic plates on a concrete floor or whack a junker car with a baseball bat or throw axes. These are things that are hard to do in the comfort and privacy of your own home because they cause the police to show up, plus the cleanup sucks and the insurance adjusters get less and less understanding as time goes by. Rage Rooms are brilliant but kind of expensive; but you can get a similar effect by visiting batting cages or going to hit a bucket of balls (or seven or eight buckets depending on the day) at a local driving range. Racquetball, bowling, pretty much any sport that involves hitting or throwing something at something else can be wildly therapeutic when you're mad as hell.

Most of us are unlikely to have our own private batting cage, racquetball or tennis court, driving range… you get the picture. A number of these sports are also seasonal in nature, which means you either have to stay mad until spring or figure out a new plan. You could call up the secretary at your local racquetball club and say, "Yes, hello, I plan on being angry as hell on Tuesday evening at about 6:30, can I reserve a court for that time please?"

I did have a thought about finding a re-breakable board (yes, this is a thing, it's a plastic board made in two pieces that 'breaks' when you hit it right. It would also probably break if you ran through it with a circular saw, but power tools don't pack the necessary anger-destroying punch.) We had one left over from when Kaiden and I used to do martial arts, but I could never break that damn thing when I was actually in training so I suspect that now I would just hurt myself badly. Or, possibly, hurt whoever got stuck holding the board, potentially inducing that person to vengeful violence. I have little desire to explain to an emergency room physician how I got the weird piece of yellow plastic stuck in my ear.

Enter the Tupperware. This stuff is amazing for its rage-destroying properties, plus it locks in freshness. You can spike it straight into a sidewalk or floor, whang it off a support pole in a basement, or just take the handy flavor-sealing lid and smack it repeatedly against a door frame while spewing curses that would make anyone hearing you want to call an exorcist. It has just enough weight to be satisfying if you throw it hard at, say, a metal garbage can (it goes CLONNNNNGGGGG!) and nobody ever has all the lids that match the versatile, non-staining, top rack dishwasher-safe food savers that come in a variety of sizes.

Also, as silly as this sounds, when you manage to break a piece of Tupperware into a zillion tiny, sharp bits you feel really badass. You're all like, "Yo, one quart salad saver? Let's see you save any salad NOW, beeyotch!" You jump up and down making gangsta hand gestures at the sad chunks of annihilated rubberized plastic you have created and yell, "S'RIGHT, bro, I brought shit DOWN on yo ass" and truly there is no finer way to resolve an anger management problem in this society. It makes me wonder things about the little shards of broken pottery that archaeologists are always finding. Was a pissed off mom required to dig up a bunch of clay, shape it into a pot, paint it with intricate designs depicting tribal life, and fire it carefully in a meticulously tended kiln over two days to bring out the colors before beating it into dust with a handy rock in a fit of preindustrial pique? Truly, we live in a magnificent age.

Jayce: Suburban Car Thievery

When I think about it, it seems strange that I was never really one to have panic attacks when I lived in my former household. However, when I arrived at the Prices' I suppose the walls came down and I found a safe place to finally crash. I was comfortable, so it was okay to cry and feel awful because I learned that nobody who really loved me would let me go through it alone.

At first when I would start to shake and go numb, I didn't really know what was happening because I wasn't familiar with feeling so out of control. There were many instances when I would beg Kaiden to go away and leave me alone and he would calmly say "Nope" and take my car keys and call Mom's parents to get me a ride back to school when the attack ended. Kaiden has always had my back and no matter how irritating I can be, he and my dad Daniel have always supported me.

An illustration of what these crises were like occurred one Sunday night when I tried to visit my parents in my old hometown. It was an utter disaster. We went to dinner, and during dinner my father was fine but my mother gave me hell. I texted Kelly and told her my mom was giving me a really hard time, so she knew what was going on. After dinner we went back to my old house, and then my former parents switched roles and now the hell was coming from my dad.

Part of the emotional trauma from that night was caused by my ex-parents' adopting of a kitten, which they had done the exact day I left home. This was clearly out of spite, because they knew very well that after the loss of my kitty a few years before I had been begging for another cat. I would talk about it every day but my parents always said it "wasn't the time." All of a sudden it apparently WAS the time, because I was replaced by a little orange and white furball. I really wanted to meet the kitty because I am an absolute sucker for cats.

Unfortunately, my former father got violent, I got shaken up, very upset and then was left alone. My ex-parents took off in their car just to drive around so they wouldn't have to deal with me. I called Kaiden, who said "Come home now." I was a wreck, but I did what I could to remain in control enough to drive back to the Prices' house.

I walked through the door, was welcomed by Kaiden and Kelly, and collapsed in a panic attack. Kaiden and Kelly didn't leave me alone no matter how much I wanted them to.

Shortly after this train wreck, I decided I wanted to get together with my former parents again. That evening ended in a very similar manner and I was once again left alone in tears. This time I called Kelly and she insisted that I not drive and came to pick me up. I did push back on this but I should have known not to argue, Kelly is nothing if not persistent. She hauled me into her van and I left my car on my ex-parents' street overnight.

I had given no thought to how I was going to retrieve the car without my former parents noticing I was on the street, but Kelly was already on it and had already called for backup. My ex-parents knew what Kelly's van looked like, so she called her friend Katy Snyder and said, "Hey Katy, you want to go steal a car with me?" Katy, who is loyal, demented in the same special way Kelly is, and generally epic, immediately said "Oh hell yeah!" and drove Kelly up in her own car, which was not one my former parents recognized. They grabbed my car and got out of there undetected.

I hadn't met this Katy Snyder at that time, but when I heard this story, I knew I liked her instantly, and sure enough she has become a good friend.

Chapter 8

Kelly: The Bullshit We're Bonding Over

Case management involves looking at a person from a holistic point of view and figuring out what they're going to need and how they're going to cope with life the way it is at a given moment. Case managers come in social work and legal assistance as well, but the type I am most familiar with is medical case management. Back in 1997 I was a home health nurse, and one of the buildings that often housed my clients was referred to at our agency as East Weirdo Corners. The appellation was unprofessional, but definitely accurate. This place was a sort of halfway house for people transitioning out of jail or some type of inpatient rehab or psychiatric facility, and rooms there were subsidized by the government so that these individuals' parole officers and caseworkers wouldn't be inconvenienced by any messy Denver traffic because most of their clients were in that one building. There was even a convenient coffee shop up the block just a bit that allowed us to sit there and sip hot beverages and finish up necessary paperwork before going home.

As the irreverent nickname of the place implies, East Weirdo Corners tended to have some interesting people on its residential roster at any given time. There were people there with drug addiction, criminal histories, and every psychiatric condition ever identified, but the weird thing was that they all seemed to live out their time there in relative peace. The place *worked*, for reasons no one could properly quantify. I would get paperwork about a new patient to see who would have a violent criminal history and who needed lab work drawn weekly. Stabbing criminally insane people with needles to make them bleed sounds like a bad idea, and not the sort of thing a second grader puts on their "When I Grow Up I Want To Be…" essays. I'd go over there and people who knew me would greet me by name and then the person I was assigned to would accept me as just part of the routine there and we'd all get along just fine.

One reason the building was successful was because among other historical attributes, it had a very old Otis elevator that required an actual elevator operator to run. It had a brass hand control with a brake on it and it was one of those places you really wish could talk and tell you all the stories it had seen. The same three or four guys ran the elevator in that building for decades, trading off shifts and talking trash in a courtly, respectful sort of way. I would go in and sign in at the desk and tell the clerk which resident I was there to see and they'd call the elevator operator on an ancient black Bakelite phone. A few minutes later this mechanical marvel would come clanking into the lobby and the operator would open the doors and then twitch the little joystick to get the floor lined up. He would then make polite conversation with you as he guided the contrivance to wherever you needed it to be, let you out, walk you to the patient's door, and knock politely. It was always an enjoyable ride, harkening back to a more genteel, slower time. However, that elevator could be a temperamental mechanical diva, and now and again it would simply quit completely.

Some of the clients at East Weirdo Corners had been hurriedly shuffled from system to system in an effort to get them out of one harried worker's hands and into those of another equally harried worker, and this often meant that things they needed to have done or dealt with didn't get accomplished. Take one guy who got discharged there from the jail, for example. I'm going to call him Dave. I don't recall what Dave had done to end up incarcerated, but somehow in the course of events he had ended up with a badly fractured leg. The medical staff at the jail set the leg and discharged him to East Weirdo Corners—without one of his shoes. In the snow. Still in the pajama pants they'd given him to wear at the county hospital. He had no available food and no way to cook any if he'd had it, no transportation to any store to buy more food, one shoe, no pants, and no pain medication, and this of course was one of the weekends when the balky old Otis in the building had decided to go on strike. Dave, not to put too fine a point on it, was screwed.

I intervened by finishing out my round for the day and hitting the thrift store and the grocery store for pants, snow boots, thick socks, peanut butter and bread, canned fruit, and cereal and milk. He didn't have a refrigerator but we stuck a bottle of milk on the window ledge outside his window and it stayed perfectly cold. The next day I called the discharge planner at the jail and turned on my very best 'I am pissed, so I am channeling Minerva McGonagall' tone. By the time I finished the conversation, they had agreed to transfer Dave to inpatient rehab until he could walk on crutches, get his pain prescription delivered to him prior to the transfer, reimburse me for my expenses, and sign off on the incident form I created about the debacle.

Dave's story is a cautionary tale on How Not To Be A Case Manager. Whoever had responsibility for him did a hell of a lot of damage by rubber stamping him on to the next person and he really suffered.

Those who are parents of kids with special needs will know what I mean when I say that it's not the child's actual care that takes most of the time. These parents spend insane amounts of time on hold with medical equipment providers, insurance companies, therapy companies, community-based funding sources for respite and camps and equipment, doctors, other doctors, special needs care coordinators who are supposed to figure all this out for you but don't, home care providers… the list goes on and on and on. It is exhausting, time consuming, backbreaking mental work and it requires the planning and logistics skills of a master chess champion. To add to the fun, these people you are constantly calling are not under your actual control, so there is nothing to prevent them from screwing up, forgetting critical information, sending the wrong supplies to the wrong place, calling in sick so you don't have nursing, changing jobs just when you've got them properly trained on how to care for your kid and are comfortable enough to let your guard down a tiny bit… that list, also, goes on and on and on. You learn to be polite and incredibly persistent, because screaming accomplishes nothing and in the end you just need your kid to be competently cared for.

Then there are layers and layers of bureaucracy. When our youngest child, Mari, came to us, we found ourselves in a situation where even with the assistance of the foster care system, which included their Guardian Ad Litem (an attorney assigned to advocate for a kid in foster care) and several caseworkers, we had a terrible time getting them on Medicaid because quite literally no one knew their name. Their birth certificate said one thing and their Social Security card said something else. Nobody knew what the truth was. The trouble was, the baby was eight weeks old and needed baby well care stuff like shots and exams and making sure they were developmentally on track, and so one day after a whole lot of hours on hold and a whole lot of fruitless wrangling I decided to just present myself at the Medicaid office. I also decided not to try to find anyone to babysit for Mari and Gabi (then three years old) while I did it.

I went in and asked to talk to Mari's caseworker, whereupon I was informed that nobody there could talk to me at all without express permission from Mari's birth mom, despite her being in foster care.

"Oh," I said. "Well, here's the number for their Guardian Ad Litem, you can call her. I'll wait." I settled myself comfortably in the waiting room with a book and two little kids.

Maybe you don't know exactly how much havoc a three-year-old can create in a waiting room, but let me tell you, it's spectacular, especially if the kid's mother (me) does absolutely nothing to curtail her. She completely destroyed all the carefully stacked piles of brochures, flyers, and magazines. She gnawed on furniture. She climbed up every chair in the place and jumped off it yelling "Mom! Watch me!" and I responded with, "Wow, you really jumped far that time!" She crawled under people's feet. Pretty soon some other parents in there who were waiting for basically the same reason I was caught on to what was going on and released their OWN toddlers to run amok, and four or five moms and I chatted in a broken mixture of English and Spanish amid phrases like, "Xavier, stop licking the doorknobs," and, "Wow, yes, it DOES get pretty dark in here if you turn off all the lights, doesn't it?"

Half an hour or so went by and finally an officious little lady with a prim mouth and a superior attitude appeared and said, "I'm sorry. The caseworker is gone for lunch and then on a home visit, she won't be back in for at least two or three more hours."

"That's okay," said I, "I brought snacks and stuff for the kids, I'll wait."

Cue bananas in the cool air registers, Goldfish crackers stomped into powder and ground into the carpeting, sticky banana fingerprints on every possible surface, and of course after snack they got bored and it turned out I also had art supplies. I didn't bring glitter glue, that would have been a hostile act in violation of the Geneva convention, but 'washable' markers, crayons, and tiny scissors for cutting up construction paper into irritating little scraps that defy all efforts to pick them up, had all been conveniently placed into my bag the day before in case of just such a need.

Miraculously for some reason it only took that caseworker about an hour to return from her 'lunch and home visit'. I don't know how we got that lucky. Perhaps someone made a phone call and expedited something, although I can't think why as we weren't raising any fuss at all. The prim little officious woman reappeared and said the caseworker would see us now. We went into the room, took three minutes to establish Mari's identity and status as a foster kid, completed one form authorizing Daniel and I to access benefits on their behalf, and were gone.

This basic scenario has been repeated several times since. It is amazingly effective for getting things done, to the point where when I know I am in for a long wait in some bureaucrat's office I am tempted to borrow someone's toddler to take with me because it is just that good.

Jayce came to us with double the case management needs, partially because his parents refused to provide him with any of his own vital documents and partially because of course his legal name at the time was not Jayce. He loathes hearing his deadname and had no desire to have anyone in my family know what it was, either. On top of the vital documents issue there were things like college financial aid applications that required his parents' tax information and getting him set up with medical care. This all resulted in my creating a document we called The Big Scary Checklist Of Logistical

Insanity. This thing read like an incident commander's disaster management strategy and it had everything on it triaged so that we could easily see what items were the highest priority and what could be put further down the list. There were literally dozens of things that needed to be done, all of which were very necessary and some of which were downright critical. Priority 1, I decided, was to get him certified copies of his birth certificate and Social Security card and to make sure he was set up financially for college so he wouldn't be dependent on the whims of his parents. The next week we started the actual Bonding Over Bullshit process using a systematic and highly organized plan called Driving All Over Hell.

Jayce: Driving All Over Hell

In the past, I have been asked "why do you want to be trans?" This is a stupid and potentially offensive question. Being trans sets you up for ostracism, violence, the loss of close relationships, and a lot of pain. Being transgender is hard. Nobody would choose this. Gender is innate, inborn, and definitely not something you change on a whim. No matter what you do to treat your dysphoria, there's still something else you wish you could change. You are insecure, self-conscious, mentally unstable in more severe cases, and hating living in your own body. No one WANTS to put themselves through surgery or a second puberty or feeling insecure every day, but if you are trans, you do what you can to get to the next day and eventually feel like yourself.

You also have to be prepared to explain why you have scars across your chest, why you look 14, or why your voice is suddenly changing dramatically and you are 19. People always want all that information, even when it's completely irrelevant or none of their business or both. You may need to tell a random doctor you've only met once why you take testosterone and hope that they understand. Unfortunately there is always a risk that they won't.

The bureaucratic bullshit alone is huge. If you change your name, you have to change everything. All identification, medical records, academic records, and practically everything that you would find your name on will need to be changed.

When you first come out, you have to tell everyone why you're changing your name and pronouns and hope for the best. Most people are terrified of coming out and that's all they think about for months. Somehow, I didn't. I didn't even think about how terrible my parents would be, but dealing with them was my most significant challenge by far. I knew who I was and ran with it.

In the very beginning there was a huge pile of things I needed to get done just to feel like myself, plus I needed to take a lot of steps to get free of my dependency on my former parents so I could start my adult life as the guy I'm supposed to be. Kelly was a huge help, she had spent years working with different social service systems and she was able to make a list of what seemed like a thousand things we had to do. Slowly, we began checking those things off, one by one. We have gotten a hell of a lot done together.

Chapter 9

Kelly: Who The Hell's Driving?

"Jayce."

No response.

"JAYCE."

Inarticulate unspellable teenage noise of distress. I took this to mean he was sentient and said, "Get up, we have shit to do."

He muttered something unintelligible that clearly contained the word 'Fuck' and rolled over and burrowed under the pillow like a hibernating ground squirrel.

"Jayce," I said, "I am extremely difficult to get rid of. You want me to go away, right? You really, really do. Instead I am going to have to sit here babbling inanities at you until I get a coherent response. I have a lot of inanities I can babble about. Shall I start with Trump, do you think? Or would you prefer to listen to babbling about 80's fashion trends? Or memes old people post on Facebook? Or shall I just babble extemporaneously? I don't need a script, you know, I can keep it up all day."

He s-l-o-w-l-y slid the pillow off his face and gave me a baleful, glassy, one-eyed glare. "Early," he said.

"It's quarter to nine. I've been up for three hours. I've folded two loads of laundry and taken the other kids to school and so get up, we're Driving All Over Hell."

"Wha—" He tried again. "—t. Wha-t. WHAT do we have to do?"

"Well," I replied cheerily, "We are driving from here to Northwest Hell to visit your old high school, and from there we are driving to Southeast Hell to get you a legal copy of your birth certificate."

He sat up at a sort of glacial speed. "Who the hell's driving?"

I looked him over carefully, noting the vacant stare and complete lack of comprehension of—or interest in—the events of the world, and my sense of self-preservation asserted itself. "Me. I'm in charge of the hell driving. You can have control of the stereo, though."

"Will there be food?" he said in a pleading tone.

"Of course," I told him. "I would never deprive you of sustenance."

Now we need to backtrack a bit in order to clarify the reasons for my plan for this particular day. Two Useful Facts will help to establish some context. Useful Fact One: Jayce was born in Russia and adopted by his parents when he was two years old. This had the potential to make getting his birth certificate a tad challenging, since when asked in what state his adoption had been finalized he looked at me and said, "Russia…" with no ability to narrow things down in the least. I thought of Omar Sharif as Dr. Zhivago, trudging through the deep snow with icicles in his mustache trying to get to his beloved Lara, and decided searching for records from all of Russia was just not a challenge I was up for that week, even with coffee, so I needed a new plan.

Useful Fact Two: Public school districts are required to maintain copies of identifying documents in a student's school records. While trying to think of a way to work around the problem that his parents had created in denying him his own birth certificate, I hit on the solution of going to his old school and having him request copies of the relevant documents, which we could then convey to the Department of Vital Records in southeast Denver along with his driver's license and hopefully obtain a certified birth certificate for him. This necessitated a total of about seventy miles of driving that morning. Jayce grabbed a can of soda and a bag of those bright red fiery Doritos snack things just in case I had lied about the food, decisively set his hat on his head backwards, and said, "Let's go." Then he remembered that he needed shoes. Whoops.

We set off in the modern equivalent of a covered wagon through the trackless unexplored territory along Colorado Highway 93 (only four lanes plus a median, barely navigable) and eventually we arrived at Jayce's old high school. On the way we listened to a whole bunch of music I had never heard before, some of which was actually pretty good even to this devotee of terrible 80's hair bands, talked about dumb stuff, and generally had a good time. Upon our arrival at this unimposing pile of nondescript suburban bricks, Jayce stopped, shook his head resignedly, and said "Man. I never thought I'd end up HERE again."

We went inside and it turned out that EVERYBODY at this school knew Jayce. Absolutely everybody. He was greeted as 'J' a couple of times, a fact that made me instantly bristle out of a newly-developed protective trans-mom instinct, but nobody used his deadname and for that I was extremely grateful. People kept saying the same thing to him: "It's good to see you smiling." This broke me all over again because apparently smiling hadn't been much of a thing for him in high school, and he is one of the most joyful people I know, so I was able to infer that he'd been very, very far down in previous days. Cue more protective Mama Bear stuff from Price, who decided that we were simply not going away until we had what we needed no matter how many toddlers I had to borrow. By some miracle, the item we needed had not been shredded and the records secretary was able to locate it, proving that the concept of a 'permanent record' that we like to threaten children with is somewhat nebulous. While we were at it, we asked his former counselor for a letter that he could use in the college financial aid office to apply for the dependency override thing he needed for college, thus expediting another part of the bullshit we needed to deal with.

As soon as we had the copy of Jayce's birth certificate in our hands we drove alllllllll the way down to Southeast Hell to try to get a certified copy. The mileage for that trip is not that bad, the issue is that there is quite literally no good way to get from the high school to Vital Records. There are roads, yes, it's just that there aren't any roads without gridlock or traffic lights every four blocks or random people wandering into the street to plant trees. We finally got there about an hour later, with Jayce sustained by his volatile mixture of spicy chips and Mountain Dew, and that was when we got completely lost.

The directions Google was able to provide me with led to this weird complex of industrial looking office buildings with extremely vague signage and nobody, apparently, around for miles. I'd been there before, so I expected vague, but it seemed as though the recent downturn in the economy had resulted in some changes to the signs on the buildings. To wit, there were none. Jayce and I sort of wandered around aimlessly looking at walls for a while. These were not attractive walls, these walls were painted in a weird sort of institutional nondescript color that wasn't gray, wasn't green, and wasn't brown. It sort of slid out of your brain as soon as you looked at it so you couldn't remember exactly what you'd just seen, instead you just got lost in a sort of mental haze of mild confusion. I think the paint color name is probably 'Meh, Who Cares?' My personal theory is that the color is being tested as part of a government mind control experiment that hopes to explore the possibilities of induced apathy in streamlining resource management. After all, if you are seeking out a government service and you are suddenly faced with a large blank wall of 'Meh' you're probably going to abandon your quest in favor of going to eat something bland and white.

***

Eventually a person of some gender and race wearing some kind of clothes and some sort of lanyard, (Meh) asked us if we were lost. I wasn't too deep under the spell of the Meh to be able to communicate, so I admitted that yes, we could use a little aid in getting to Vital Records, please. Apparently the lanyards confer some sort of immunity to the Meh, like maybe some sort of AntiMeh aromatherapy essential oil thing. We actually got pointed to a building with a sign on the front that very clearly said *Colorado Department of Vital Records*. That sign had NOT been there on any of the other three trips we had made past that building. That's my story and I am sticking to it.

The interior of the building was painted in Meh Interior Flat Latex, but I fought it off bravely and headed toward a big sign (mercifully) that said we were in the right place. Ten minutes later we'd obtained our certified copy of Jayce's birth certificate and were on our way to get food, only a little of which was bland and white.

Jayce: Tour of Hell

I never thought that I'd actually have fun running errands. Ever. When I was a child, I had to be dragged out of the house and you typically had to bribe me with candy, a new toy, or money. Anything. However, for the first time with Kelly, we had a hell of a good time talking in the car, singing off-key to terrible music, and eating trans chips (Spicy Doritos, we'll explain why they're called trans chips later).

We had quite a few things to do that day, so we started by going to what Kelly called "Northwest Hell," all the way from Arvada. We arrived at my old high school to try and get a copy of my birth certificate because I wasn't allowed to leave my ex-parents' house with any of my vital documents.

I had gotten a serious case of deja vu the second that I walked through the door. Wow, I never thought I'd be back there and I was hoping that nothing would bring me back, because although I made some good friends and a lot of nice memories, high school was also hell. I lost some of the best friends I ever had because guess what? I became the target of administration, and my former mother sabotaged my relationships. I still have nightmares that the counselors are going to take my current best friends away from me.

Everyone also knew me. Everyone. I'd graduated almost a year previously and all of the seniors and underclassmen somehow still knew who I was. The office staff and counselors seemed to be welcoming but I still had everything that they had put me through playing in the back of my head.

It turned out we were lucky to have gotten what we came for. They were supposed to shred all identification of former students but out of pure dumb luck, they still had mine on file. So that saved us a lot of trouble. Of course, it wasn't all going to be that easy, but we had accomplished the first mission of the day and it was onto the next.

We left "Northwest Hell" to go to "Southeast Hell" to get a certified copy. I believe it was somewhere in Aurora. It had been quite a while since my mom had a good reason to go to a vital records office, so we drove around aimlessly and toured all the parking lots in the area for a while. All of the buildings looked the same but we finally figured out where to go. Good thing we weren't on a schedule that day. We had dedicated the whole day to Driving All Over Hell.

Anyhow, when it was time to be called to the window at Vital Records, this is when it became momentarily painful. Everything was still in my given legal name, so having to show identification that didn't match my name I had chosen for myself, always made me die inside a little. All of my documents now read "male" and my name is now legally changed, so this torture is no longer a reality. I am now comfortable mentioning my deadname because we seem to meet a ridiculous number of people with this name, so now I just laugh. My mom likes to joke that I'm going to end up married to somebody with my deadname. However, at the time, it was a painful experience to appear as someone that I wasn't. Just hearing the name made my stomach drop through the floor and I would feel awful the rest of the day. My mom and I joke about how that name used to be pronounced "Yecch" because that's how it felt.

Once that whole process at the office that day was over, it was time to conclude our adventure with what was truly important: Food. Getting my ass dragged out of bed at the crack of dawn (8:45) required a lunch bribe. We were both glad to have gotten a chunk of the crap we had to accomplish out of the way, even though we surely were going to have to put up with more bullshit. It truly never ends, but at that moment, we were able to forget all of that and dine on Panera Bread.

Chapter 10

Kelly: Billiards, Basketball, and Crochet

One cannot simply plow through the bullshit involved in daily life with a transgender teen boy without having some fun. Gratuitous drudgery is everywhere and the goal of not drowning in a mixture of toil and screams is a worthy one. Of course, different people have different ideas about what constitutes fun, and in our household we have quite a crazy quilt of things that people like to do to keep themselves off the streets and (sort of) out of trouble.

I am a crochet artist. I can make really strange things out of yarn, and I especially enjoy a crochet form called amigurumi. This is a Japanese word that combines *ami*, which means yarn, with *nuigurumi*, which means 'stuffed doll'. So, literally, stuffed dolls/animals/whatever, made of yarn. I made an entire set of ornaments for our Christmas tree that are Star Wars characters. Yoda looks a little squashed and eccentric because he was the first one I ever did. Darth Vader looks like a poodle. Han Solo, Luke Skywalker, and Princess Leia look like they have had a long afternoon at the optometrist's office because I ran out of eyeballs that were the right size, said to hell with it, and put in bigger ones. If you look at them long enough you start to feel hypnotized, like you've been staring too long at the crazy cartoon snake from *The Jungle Book* (the old cartoon one, not the current version) with the spinning eyeballs singing, "Trussssst in me... Jussssst in me..." The best ones are Chewbacca, who looks exactly like Chewbacca should, and Darth Maul, who I did without a pattern and who required crazy ingenuity to get right. I have also made a bunch of dragons, a Blue-Footed Booby, an okapi, some eccentric little mice, Legolas from *Lord Of The Rings* (for which I feel I owe Orlando Bloom an apology), Frank N Furter from *The Rocky Horror Picture Show*, Trillian from *The Hitchhiker's Guide To The Galaxy,* and assorted other funky little characters. Last year I won a bet with a friend by making a piano that actually plays music using a little music box inside it. It's fun stuff. There are a lot of useful patterns out there, you can make the little girl from *The Exorcist* complete with yarn projectile barf, Lin Manuel Miranda from *Hamilton*, you name it.

Daniel makes cryptic crossword puzzles. He's on his third book of these crazy things, which take regular crosswords and turn them on their heads by making each clue into a word puzzle in and of itself. This means instead of just trying to figure out what a six-letter word for sheep is, you have to figure out what the person creating the puzzle did with the words that make the clue and then from there figure out what the answer is. These things are so diabolical that one of the first creators was a guy who went by the name Torquemada. They have a whole set of specific rules about how words can be used and what each combination of words might mean, including anagrams, indicators, deletions, hidden words, you name it. I do not understand how people who solve—or who create—these things think. If you're interested, though, go out to http://www.excruciverbiage.com and look at *Excruciverbiage*, which is the name of Daniel's puzzle book series. The cover art was done by yours truly, with a lot of help from Kaiden's fifteen-year-old friend Ian, and I am rather proud of it.

The other kids do other stuff to keep entertained, from role-player gaming to drawing comics to skiing. None of them has a particularly refined thing they have stuck to over time. Instead, in the typical manner of kids, they bounce from activity to activity doing whatever stuff grabs their interest. And Jayce is a musician and singer, recording artist and he loves to make really complicated things out of Legos. He also enjoys making me look stupid on the basketball court, which I repay by making him look stupid at the pool table.

Jayce: I'm alright at pool. Shut up.

I am one of those people who cannot be still. The only time I stop moving is when I'm asleep. I'm also not a quiet person. Most of the stuff I like to do for fun, therefore, involves either physical activity or making noise.

I make good noise, not just random noise, although I make a fair amount of that too. I'm a singer and a songwriter and I know a lot about sound design. I've got a couple of albums I created and I've done some performing as well. In the winter of 2019, my parents held a salon concert in their living room with artist Jane Siberry that was a lot of fun – I got to be her opening act.

I also really like kids, and even though I am a grownup I have a great time playing card games and basketball and riding trick scooters with my younger siblings and with kids in the neighborhood. I have always needed a lot of physical activity, and I'll get involved in any sport I'm invited to play.

One really cool thing that has happened is that now I like to swim. Going in a pool used to cause a lot of dysphoria, because I couldn't just wear swim trunks like any other boy. Now I can and I love letting my mom shove me into the pool and throwing a foam football with my dad. I have a great time.

Chapter 11

Kelly: Siblings. A lot of them. All at once.

"I always wanted younger siblings," said Jayce on the ride home the day we moved him in.

I cast him a side-eyed glance and said, "Oh really? Do tell…"

"Yeah. I always thought I would make a good big brother," he said. Foreshadowing here, this is one of those 'be careful what you wish for' situations. Jayce now finds himself with not one, not two, but three younger siblings. We're not quite the Brady Bunch, because we have infinitely better fashion and interior decorating sense, and all the males in the house have better hair, but there are parallels.

Having Baby #1 was something of a shock, because Kaiden was born so early and so sick, but we did know we wanted him and he was loved and cared for from the first minute he was alive.

People kept trying to warn me about what life would be like after going from one kid to two kids, but nothing prepares you for the actual fact. Raising the first kid through babyhood and young childhood was sort of like trying to ride up Mt. Everest on a tricycle. There is a hell of a lot of mountain above you most of the time, and your wheels keep slipping in this unnerving way, and you just never quite get to stop pedaling. In Kaiden's case there were therapies, feeding tubes, and my best friend Lactina, the breast pump (we were super tight, Lactina and I).

Adding Gabi to the family was a special adventure in Himalayan Mountain Tricycling because she was on oxygen and a feeding pump at the time she arrived with us. She took the oxygen out of her nose 38,263,462 times a night, and then she would turn blue and her oxygen saturation number would drop dangerously. Fortunately, she was on a monitor for this, so for me, peacefully sleeping while she desaturated into organ failure wasn't a thing that was going to happen. Invariably when she took the oxygen out of her nose she would just sort of flick it upwards and it would be blowing on her eyebrows, which were not the breathing part of her face—I learned that in nursing school. The other thing she'd do was to stick it in her mouth because she liked to feel the bubbles on her tongue. The alarm on the monitor would go 'Beebeebeep, beebeep'. It played the MOST annoying intrusive little tune, which I am certain was so that I would pay attention to it and fix whatever version of Gabi-lung-disease drama was causing her numbers to drop.

I quite literally did not sleep more than an hour at a stretch for six months. Unfortunately, the average time for a sleeper to complete the full cycle of four stages of quiet sleep and then REM sleep is about ninety minutes, so all those restorative benefits of good sleep were not a thing in my world. The first time I got a stretch of three hours I felt *terrific*, like I could run a marathon or two. It was AMAZING. In general, though, I kind of wandered through that first year in a fog, needing to write down absolutely everything and hoping that Kaiden wouldn't have some kind of crisis because I just didn't have the bandwidth to cope with it.

Going from two kids to three kids was also something of an adventure, because Mari was one of those babies who liked to scream about food a lot. They were pretty sure they were never, ever getting fed again, and that if they could have just held a phone in their pudgy little hand they would have called CPS immediately and reported us for being four minutes late with the formula. Mari was also really weird for me because they ate like a normal kid, and the other two had been tube-fed their whole lives. Tube-fed kids are an exercise in the complex mathematics of nutrition. Someplace there is a dietician with a calculator counting out grams of protein and fat and making sure that the baby is receiving the appropriate amounts of vitamins, minerals, and essential amino acids for their age. You can drive yourself absolutely insane trying to work on the details of a tube feeding plan that optimizes your kid's nutritional intake so that it's better than that of an Ironman triathlete, and all the while other kids around you are dunking Cheetos into maple syrup and calling it breakfast. I remember one clinic appointment with Mari soon after they came home with a weird nostalgic bemused feeling because I asked the nurse practitioner how I could tell they were getting enough food and she peered at me over her reading glasses and said, "Well, they're not shrieking, right?" The revelation that babies are born with built in alarm systems that cause them to hit 110 decibels when they're a quart low was quite eye-opening for me, which was really dumb considering how long I'd been in nursing.

This was also when my coffee addiction was born. I had worked night shift for ten years and raised two kids past babyhood and I never drank coffee. The weather that day was cold and spitting snow, and I had taken the older two kids to their respective schools and decided to hit Starbucks for a cup of hot chocolate. Mari, in their baby seat, predictably began to scream, so I was a tiny bit tense sitting in the drive through line. I got to the speaker and a tinny little friendly voice said, "Good morning, welcome to Starbucks, what can I make for you today?" and I burst into hysterical tears and had to pull up to the window so I could order coherently over the howling from the back seat. I asked for cocoa and a cup of warm water to mix some baby formula and the barista looked at me, noted the fact that literally everyone in my van was sobbing, said, "Oh no, honey, drink this" and handed me a mocha.

My God it was a miracle. Suddenly I was sharp, organized, on top of things, with energy to spare. Laundry got caught up, the house got cleaned, some errands happened, and all this was accomplished in the two and a half hours that Gabi was in preschool. This coffee stuff, it was the elixir of the gods! Sure, it tasted totally nasty unless I added a whole bunch of stuff to it to turn it into a dessert, but wow did it ever make me feel amazing!

Anyhow, back to Jayce and his three little siblings. "Be careful what you ask for" indeed.

He and Kaiden are three years apart in age and super tight. Kaiden is this loyal kid who takes Jayce's side in absolutely everything and who adores him in an unconditional way that allows him to be completely himself. The two of them watch sitcoms together and talk about life a lot. Kaiden is trans male and is active with his school's gay/straight alliance so he already has a lot of friends who identify in ways other than cisgender and straight. He's an includer in the biggest way.

Occasionally Jayce forgets that he was raised by wolves and shows Kaiden an R-rated movie or, on one memorable occasion, a French movie. Okay, yeah, French movies can be cool, especially if you are an adolescent male. I admit that at my current age I watched most of the film while thinking about crochet patterns, but that is no reflection on my beleaguered husband. Anyway, this particular French movie involves a girl figuring out she likes to sleep with other girls, and this requires two hours and change plus a lot of sex scenes to accomplish. The kids found this riveting. Much discussion ensued over which of the girls was hotter and how many takes it required to get a given scene shot and whether or not all that enthusiasm was authentic or just acting. I could hear a director in my head going, "Okay, now let's try that again, except just a little to the left and slightly more tongue, and can you moan in the direction of the boom mic, please?" and imagine the girls rolling their eyes and thinking about lunch breaks. I admit to being jaded and cynical, as well as old.

Kaiden is also the kid who won't hesitate to come get me if Jayce needs me at night to help him cope with a panic episode or drive him to the crisis center or whatever he needs. Jayce himself will come upstairs and peer into our bedroom and decide I need my sleep. Then he will go downstairs and pick holes in his skin with his nails or damage himself in some other way all alone. Kaiden is hardheaded and practical and knows well that I would much prefer being awakened to deal with things than to allow anyone to be miserable all alone. He's fought his own psychiatric demons and he understands through experience that little wins add up to big wins.

Gabi loves Jayce completely. I mean she *adores* him. For Christmas this year he made each member of the family a CD that has his music on it, and I don't believe Gabi has listened to anything else since then. She has a gift for seeing him the way he wants to see himself, as just a guy, and she accepts him wholeheartedly even with all his foibles and quirks. She's got her own share of foibles and quirks to cope with, given her health issues and status as an adoptee.

That said, she has a tendency to say exactly what is on her mind at any given moment. Which brings me to a story.

We were attending an annual dinner at a local high school that is called *Empty Bowls*. The upshot is that people donate crockpots full of soup and chili and everyone eats together. The event raises money for our local food bank, as well as promoting awareness of the food needs of our community. It's a fun evening, the elementary school orchestra performs and the choir sings and a lot of the teachers from area schools attend with their families.

Everyone got soup and then Gabi took Jayce over to introduce him to her art teacher, which she did by saying, "This is my brother, Jayce. He's trans." So much for tact or discretion, right? Anyway, this abrupt outing caused a complete collapse of Jayce's emotional Jenga game and hysteria ensued. I hauled both kids into the hallway for a discussion about how you don't just tell people personal shit on first acquaintance and I demanded that Gabi apologize to Jayce immediately, which being a snarky little tween she refused to do.

At this point Kaiden decided to get involved. He's considerably unmotivated by a need to handle his sister diplomatically and he got very direct. "That was DUMB, Gabi, and was totally NOT okay. You don't just say stuff like that. You need to say you're sorry and *right now*."

This finally got through to Gabi, who after all had never intended to injure her much beloved older brother, and she started to sob out of a combination of embarrassment and remorse. Which triggered a nosebleed.

So now I had one outed eighteen-year-old in tears, one nine-year-old in tears (with blood!), and one very irritated fifteen-year-old. The only sane course of action was to abandon our soup and leave, still hungry and still in full Soap Opera Mode (with blood!) I did try to explain that for Gabi having people in her life who are transgender is a completely normal thing and therefore she saw no reason to keep it hidden. This caused Jayce and Kaiden to get annoyed with me because they saw it as my responsibility to educate the younger kids about when—and when not—to disclose somebody's gender identity. (Dude. I tried. These kids are a work in progress.)

Anyhow, Gabrielle can shriek like a firebell when she's feeling put out, and the noise she was making set Mari off in the car, and the screaming continued the whole way home. Eventually everyone got calmed down and peace was restored, but it was one of those life lessons in unconditional love where you learn that people aren't perfect and we're all in this together.

This drama aside, Gabi is probably the most totally loving of the three O.P.G.'s (Original Price Gangstas) where Jayce is concerned. He can do nothing wrong in her eyes. When she is upset and needs comforting, he throws himself into the job without the slightest hesitation, which we call 'Doing Your Brother Thing'. He can get her to do stuff, too, like help clean up or put groceries away, that I haven't got a prayer of getting her to do. This is a lesson in Shamelessly Using One Kid To Help Raise Another and is the reason moms who have four or more kids actually have less stress in their lives than moms of three.

Mari at age 8 totally 'gets' things in this hilarious eight-year-old way that is incredibly wise. Mari tested seriously gifted and reads at roughly a sixth-grade level, and they read everything they can get their hands on whether it's appropriate for their age or not. After the aforementioned episode at the *Empty Bowls* event, Mari reflected for a few minutes and said sagely, "You know, you have to treat transgender people gently. Like animals. Except you don't pet them like dogs." Mari has a nametag that reads *Jaycequake, Trauma, Panic and Flashback Assistant* because they discovered that when Jayce goes into panic mode it helps him to hang out with them. They're incongruous with the things he's having flashbacks about—his brain goes, "Wait, I never had a Mari in my life when these things were happening, this must not be real..." and he resets. It's kinda brilliant, honestly. Mari is a grounding influence and they really, really like feeling like they're helping.

Plus, they're cute. Mari is a bouncy, silly, little goof with huge brown eyes and brown hair, and at the time of this writing is missing their two front teeth. They're a typically adorable little kid. They'll lisp out a request for Jayce to play with them or read to them or whatever and he just caves. Jayce and Mari share a series of inside jokes that cause the rest of us to roll our eyes and sigh a lot. They laugh about why Mari is not allowed to watch Desperate Housewives and torment the cats.

This all helps balance things out when Mari is annoying. They will occasionally go up to him and sort of stare at him just for the hell of it. They'll bounce up and down on their toes, staring at him, not making any noise, and he tries to ignore them and hopes they'll go away, and when they don't, he looks at me and goes, "Mari is being annoying." Whereupon I say, "Oh really? Huh..." It's kind of fun to watch all this happen, for me.

Having Jayce arrive the way he did caused all the kids in the family to kind of gang together in this cemented way that makes them all closer. This is not to say they never fight about anything. Kaiden and Gabi are especially prone to sniping at one another over trivialities, because one mouthy tween and one exasperated, jaded teen makes for a slightly volatile combination, but they all know that if you're a Price kid, you have all the REST of the Price kids standing with you no matter what. When they all have to get together for a conversation about What To Do About Mom when I am old and can no longer reliably drive myself anyplace or cook anything, I am pretty sure they'll manage to work together.

Jayce: And You Get To Keep Them

Overall, I am really glad to have siblings. They make my life much better. I have discovered, though, that like in any family, they can drive you absolutely batshit. There are a lot of times we switch in seconds from being at each other's throats to laughing and having fun and ganging up on Mom and Dad, which I know they secretly appreciate. One minute Mari and I might be yelling at each other, the next minute we will be laughing like idiots because we're both wearing the same clothes. When I am playing a card game with Mari or calming them down, or I have Gabi in my arms or Kaiden next to me, I feel incredibly lucky to be their brother. Life is much better with them, than without.

In the beginning we went through a kind of honeymoon phase where we were pretty much perfect in each other's eyes. We couldn't see any conflict down the road. Instead it turned out we are actually a normal family, and there is conflict and there are things we have to deal with together.

One event that falls under the "Everything will be funny eventually" category is that Empty Bowls dinner. When Gabi introduced me as trans I was still in that overly self-conscious and self-critical stage you get into when your dysphoria is not quite treated. I was pre-T and pre-surgery at that point so anything that came up that made me feel less like myself set me off.

It was also the first time I had a significant conflict with any of my siblings. I was kind of surprised. I said "Mom, didn't you teach her better than this?" and Mom said "Well, I tried." At that moment it was genuinely awful, I was just trying to live my life as a guy without everyone thinking about how I identified.

When we got in the car it was tears and hysterics all around and I could just picture Dad's brain going "OMG, these are my children, now what do I do?" Mari's comic relief about how you don't pet trans people like dogs was desperately needed.

Gabi now finds this story extremely embarrassing. The rest of us all think it is extremely funny. I think that's a good sign.

Sibling relationships can also be hard because in my old life I was an only child with a trauma background, so I just lived every day hoping to survive it and get on to the next. I didn't grow up having to share, but I also didn't get what I needed, which has brought a competitive fire into my personality. Sometimes I feel I need to compete with my siblings for resources or status or power. I will decide I want to win a game just to feel empowered for those five minutes when it's over.

My parents have started to get through to me the idea that these kids will be my family forever and that I need to let that five minutes of power go by if I want thirty more years of connection with the people in my family that I love.

Chapter 12

Kelly: Friends Old And New

We have now forcibly pried Jayce free of his abusive home situation with the Crowbar Of Love and the Winch Of Family, but now we get to discuss friendships and connections and who is still part of his life and how he's staying connected to them. The object of this game was not to isolate Jayce from all his old connections, it was to keep him safe and protected. He's an extremely extroverted kid and he has a lot of friends.

However, in some instances, this adventure is exactly like a divorce. Which means the friends (and extended family) have to play a game called *Whose Side Are You On?* Which party 'gets' which friends after a family split is always a contentious question, and this is no different in Jayce's case.

I will start with the Kennedys. Brian, Vivian, and their three kids are a seriously awesome and incredibly close-knit family who support each other in the most amazing ways and always have. Despite being flung across the nation for college (Isabelle is in Boston, Charlie at Stanford, and Peter at Lehigh) they all manage to stay tightly woven together.

Jayce says now that when he met the Kennedys he had this 'oh, wow' kind of revelation watching them interact. He wanted his family to be like that, too. He didn't honestly know that the Kennedy family are actually relatively normal: they enjoyed their kids, there were forts and trees to climb in their back yard, they went camping and hiking and took family vacations together, played games, watched movies, and the kids ran amok in a genial sort of free-spirited way in their neighborhood.

Peter is the youngest. When he was little, he adored trains, loved them obsessively. If you went over to their house you got a detailed synopsis of which train was going where and how they all got put together and what they were carrying and what each little man in the ever-changing railyard of Peter's mind was doing. You would think as an adult that you might get bored and start going, "Yes, Peter, that's cool" in this sort of bland 'I'm not really listening I'm just humoring you' sort of way, but Peter had a knack for pulling you into the world of his trains with him and making you suspend disbelief.

When he was a little bit older, he briefly held the world record for cup stacking. Probably you have seen this, it is a thing where kids take plastic cups and stack them into different shapes and sizes of pyramids very fast. If you haven't seen it, go look, it's fun to watch and you will think you want to try it yourself. Peter was very, very fast at this.

He's a kind, warm-hearted, sweet kid. I can still picture him at about age three, eating dinner with us, and suddenly he flung his arms around Brian, laid his head against him and said, "Daddy, do I make you happy?"

Brian hugged him tightly and said, "Yes, you make me happy. I wish you wouldn't HIT people, but you definitely make me happy."

Peter and Jayce met one day on a bike ride and decided they should hang out together, and Jayce sees this as a major turning point in his life. Peter reached out and scooped Jayce into his circle and Jayce started seeing possibilities for his future that he'd never even thought about before. This, of course, caused more friction in Jayce's home life as he worked to figure out who he was and find his footing on a path in life.

Jayce's chosen middle name is Kennedy in honor of the people who opened up his world so much. He says he owes Peter his life, and he isn't kidding about that.

Anna and Chiara Pesce have both grown up with parents who have worked like crazy to support the girls in exploring their passions. Both are professional caliber dancers; Anna with a troupe called the Silhouettes who performed on America's Got Talent, go find them online, they're absolutely mind-blowing. Chiara is a very accomplished Irish step dancer who travels frequently with her dance school and who is completely confident in herself in ways that are very mature for her age. Their mom, Michelle, is an absolute rock when it comes to supporting her girls and her schedule reads like a Tetris game.

Anna and Jayce bonded over a date.

I had spent some time thinking about Jayce and dating and the issues that come up there, and one day I hit on the idea of introducing them. They're somewhat alike, have some similar interests, and I knew Anna would be completely at ease with Jayce's transgender status. Plus she's absolutely drop dead beautiful. I showed Jayce some pictures of her on Facebook and his eyes just about rolled out of his skull. I got in touch with Michelle and we set up a meeting for the kids, and the moms went also to drink coffee and hang out and chat.

Now, my sweet boy has a touch of ADHD, and that combined with a case of nerves about the date had him royally wound up. To add to this, that day I had had the conversation with him that all parents of boys need to have when their kid starts dating, to wit: How You Treat A Young Lady. I started with the usual things, respect, good manners, curfews and restrictions, not driving like a bat out of hell, the usual stuff. As I went through my lecture Jayce's eyes kept getting bigger and bigger and finally I stopped and looked at him and said, "What? Why are you staring at me all bug-eyed like that?"

"Wow," he said sort of breathlessly, "I've never. Never been actually encouraged. To date a girl. Like, a real girl. On a date. With a girl. This is weird."

Michelle, me, and the teenagers met at a local coffeehouse and Jayce got instantly and totally starstruck over Anna and as soon as a different table opened up the two of them ditched us to go talk alone. I have some photos from that night, and in every last one of them Jayce appears blurry. He's not exactly a paragon of stillness under normal circumstances, but that night, the boy was completely red-shifted talking to Anna. He was absolutely berserk with joy.

Michelle was watching this with a sort of bemused cautious expression. "He's... a lot," she told me.

The kids eventually agreed to go on a second date. This one made me laugh because it was very carefully planned by both of them as an experiment. First, to see if they had romantic chemistry. Second, as a practice date (With a girl! A real girl! This is weird...) for Jayce. I knew with certainty that Anna would be completely straight with him about how he handled himself on a date. If he wasn't well-mannered, she'd let him have it.

They also agreed to deconstruct the date. They said, "Okay, we're going to do this, and then we will have an analysis. And that is exactly what they did. They sat in her driveway going, "How do you think that went?" and they exchanged information and suggestions and agreed that they're better as friends. Romantic chemistry aside, they decided they needed to have some kind of relationship that would actually outlast the whole teenage whirlwind romance dating bullshit thing that kids do, and so now they're tight buddies, completely free to date other people, and happy about that.

Jayce has archived thousands of texts from Anna. He can look back on everything they have ever said to one another. It's like a demented sort of diary. "Hey Jayce, what happened on December 3?" and he can scroll back and say, "Oh, that was the first day I ended up at the crisis center, wow that sucked."

He swears he has archived texts from everyone. I think that was meant as some kind of disclaimer.

I never quite know how people from Jayce's past are going to respond to me. Usually, he tells an abbreviated form of the story and people go "Wow…" and then the Price family gets introduced to them and life is good. A couple of times there have been awkward moments when people have had to figure out how to react to such a huge change, and on occasion someone just friends me on Facebook because they're happy that Jayce is thriving in his new habitat. Once in a while, though, there's a different reaction, because people are not in possession of all the facts in Jayce's history. They decide that he did an evil thing by renouncing his old name and leaving his family, and that I abetted him in this solely to do harm.

One afternoon I ended up getting introduced to the father of an old friend of Jayce's that he no longer has much contact with. He's sad about this, he and that particular friend were really close at one time and he misses her.

It didn't occur to me at the time that this guy might not like me, and when I said "Hi, nice to meet you" there was an instant open hostility that took me by surprise. I felt like a Disney-type curse had been placed on me, you know, of the "A pox on you and yours" sort. During the short conversation that followed he was extremely rude, interrupting and holding up fingers and literally going "Tut tut!" at me when I'd try to speak. I was too bewildered to be angry at the time, and then when I thought it over I realized that this guy had heard only one side of Jayce's story – that of his former parents. I decided that I probably wouldn't like me either under those circumstances.

In another awkward conversation, a lady who had known Jayce's family well told me she had thought of calling the police when Jayce left home and moved in with us. This thought came to her in spite of the fact that Jayce was 1.) legally an adult, and 2.) leaving of his own volition and by his own free will. Apparently, we are not only a cult, we are also kidnappers. I imagined the police showing up at my door and tasing my kids while another cop said helpful, soothing things to my son, like "We'll get you out of here, young lady, you're safe now."

Jayce: More Love Is Better

Mom always says this, and it definitely applies to me when I think about the friends I have made and the friends I have left. When I came to the Prices, I didn't have a whole lot of friends or people I knew. The people I was still consistently in touch with from my old life included the Kennedys, and it still blows my mind how pivotal that bike ride with Peter was. I met Peter in Social Studies class in my sophomore year in high school. I didn't really know anything about him except for his name, and I didn't even have that right. I thought his first name was Kennedy because that's what our teacher always called him. I got the idea that he was a really kind, polite kid who might make a good friend when we partnered on a school project.

I was out for a bike ride one day after a rough afternoon with my old family. I was just looking to escape for a while, and Peter recognized me. He Snapchatted me and we discovered we lived in the same neighborhood. We got together the next day and the rest is history.

The first time I heard about my other best friend, Anna, was when her mother, Michelle, loaned me the boxes I used when I moved out. Her daughter has become one of my closest friends. My mom introduced us at a local coffee shop, and I asked Anna out, and it blew my mind that an actual, living, breathing girl wanted to go out with me. I had seen her picture on Facebook and let's just say she was pretty. When I asked to meet her, I had a conversation about dating etiquette with my mom, and so I followed all the rules about treating her respectfully and getting her home on time because I wanted Anna to at least think I wasn't a Neanderthal. The coffee shop trip was a fun night, we made a natural connection and we were friends in an hour.

We decided to go out again, this time on an actual date. We hadn't put a label on our relationship yet, so I texted her and made some suggestions.

"Here's what we're gonna do," I said. "We're gonna go out, and talk about it, and you're gonna tell me everything I did wrong." That made her laugh out loud in the middle of her English class. We did go out about a week later and decided our relationship would go furthest if we stayed friends. Meeting her was a great experience.

Some interactions we had with other former friends of mine were less pleasant. I had known one girl for maybe five or six years. We had been really close and she was part of my Jewish community and our families spent time together and had Passover and it was a nice relationship. As soon as things went downhill with my family life, we disconnected and our years of friendship didn't seem to matter anymore. I was still friendly with her parents, although we hadn't talked for a while.

Kelly and I went up to my former temple for a meeting and we ran into her dad. He was not polite to Kelly at all, but he only had one side of the story and all he knew about Kelly was that she had pretty much taken me away from my old family. If I had been him, I would have thought the same.

I still miss their family and it's unfortunate that I don't have that relationship now. I'm making up for it by keeping friends like Peter and Anna around, people I will probably know and love for the rest of my life. Hopefully there will be more to come.

Chapter 13

Kelly: A Black Sense Of Humor

Nurses see a lot of people who are not at their best. Things like civilized behavior and good manners kind of go out the window when people are doing things like waking up from anesthesia, sleeping off a drunk, or having a baby. We get barfed on and peed on and nobody ever says, "Oh pardon me, I am so sorry, that was rude, please let me pay your cleaning bill."

Years ago, there was a bed on the market for patients with mobility issues that was designed to prevent bedsores. This thing was called a Clinitron and it was a bed that contained several hundred pounds of very fine sand that was 'air fluidized', which meant that a lot of air was blown through the sand at high speed, causing it to sort of 'float' in the bed and thus the patient was supported on a cloud of sandy air. The beds made noise and cost a whole lot of cash in electric bills, but they did help with the pressure sores people got. One feature of this bed was that if you turned off the air the sand immediately settled out and became very hard, which was necessary because it is impossible to do CPR on an air fluidized bed if your patient codes.

I once took care of a patient in home health who had one of these things. He had been a gangbanger and a drug dealer and had gotten shot when a deal went hideously awry, but he continued to run his little empire from his bed despite being a quadriplegic. Which goes to show you that with enough determination you, too, could be a horizontal kingpin, but I digress.

Anyway, this guy had one of these beds in his house.

Now, the sand was contained in the bed by this sandproof sheet that kind of went over the whole thing and was supposed to be tightly secured to the bed, and if you don't see this as foreshadowing you are not paying attention.

The gentleman in question, aside from being a model citizen and a real pillar of society, had contracted some sort of intestinal ailment that resulted in intractable diarrhea for a couple of days. Needless to say, the combination of diarrhea and quadriplegia necessitated some extra assistance in keeping clean and dry, so we were kept quite busy with his daily care needs for a while. I was there with him alone one morning when one of these episodes occurred, and as I was turning him over to clean him up the damn sheet popped completely off the Clinitron bed and we were both immediately engulfed in a cloud of blowing sand that would have shocked a Bedouin.

I said some very unprofessional words and slapped the button to stop the air flow, and the sand immediately settled to the bed (and the floor.) My patient – still not cleaned up – sort of half disappeared under a third of a ton of sand.

There was nothing for it but to dive in there with him and yank him out of there, which I immediately did. Florence Nightingale—who never had to contend with anything like this— (yeah, yeah, Crimean War, whatever…) would have been proud. Use your imagination, though, and mentally conjure up an image of a gigantic cat litter box that hadn't been cleaned for a really long time. Imagine that the kitty who is unfortunate enough to have this box for a potty has been quite ill. Now add an image of two people sort of swimming in the cat box. These imaginary people are not gracefully gliding across the top of the cat box, no, they are people who are genuinely at risk of drowning. They are right down in the sand and the poo, flailing desperately for dear life and trying to keep their heads above… well, not water.

Eventually, I extricated my patient by dint of sheer insane desperation and was able to look around the room a bit. There was poo sand on every surface in the room, poo sand in our hair, poo sand in our eyebrows, and about this time the aide who was responsible for most of his daily care showed up.

"What the hell happened?" she said in aghast tones.

"The goddamn bed exploded." I gave her fifteen bucks and sent her to the nearest thrift store to buy me any item of clothing that would fit me and a towel. We got the patient up and into the shower and I cleaned him up there and installed him in a recliner in the living room and then I went and showered in his bathroom myself and dressed in the new clothes my aide friend had bought me. The outfit consisted of a dress in a style called Midcentury Bag Lady and which made me look like one of those damask pillows realtors scatter around when they're trying to sell a house. Carol Burnett would have been proud to be seen in this dress in her Scarlett O'Hara sketch. It even had a lace collar that looked like a doily had somehow come to parasitic, sentient, terrifying life. It was an absolute abomination in fabric, but it did have the redeeming quality of NOT being covered in poo sand, so I threw away my other clothes and donned it anyway, because dignity is overrated.

At the time of the occurrence, this tale of woe was not funny in the least, but I have the sort of brain that stores things up to tell people later, and recounting it over coffee with another nurse friend had both of us laughing so hard we nearly peed. We were red-faced, teary and hysterical, and people in the restaurant we were at were glaring at us, but we had lost all control and just had to surrender to gales of giggles.

Back to Jayce. He's on a safety plan (more about that in a subsequent chapter) that requires that he wake me up at night if he finds that he doesn't feel safe to be alone, either because the trauma flashbacks have got hold of his brain or because he's feeling suicidal or both. Picture this: traumatized kid comes upstairs in the middle of the night, rouses me (not the easiest task) and says he needs me downstairs. I *never* tell him no he doesn't, let me sleep. Never ever. I get my ass out of bed, doff my sexy Darth Vader CPAP mask, and head downstairs. Usually at this point Jayce has succumbed to another case of the shakes and is sort of hyperventilating and so I do my Mama Bear thing and wrap around him like a large, warm, furry, comforting thing, (yeah, I said furry, so what?) and usually after a few minutes he calms down and tells me what brought me downstairs on whichever fine evening this is.

You would think, wouldn't you, that making a lot of soothing noises at him like you would do with a skittish horse would be part of the plan, and admittedly it sort of is, but on almost every occasion one of us says something really sarcastic and incredibly inappropriate and the other one loses it completely and breaks down into snorting attempts to sort of whisper-giggle so we don't wake the whole damn household. Jayce can go from feeling really awful to unhinged giggling in about 3.2 seconds. It's a trait that is self-protective and that I quite admire, partially because it has helped him so much in the past and partially because it is one I share.

Here is an example, and I warn you if you are triggered by mentions of sexual assault you might want to skip to the next chapter and go read about deconstructing mindfulness for teenagers in the next chapter instead.

Processing some of the things Jayce has dealt with has resulted in a need on his part to know precisely what the legal definitions are of certain acts, along with the attendant circumstances surrounding those acts. Many of these things concern what constitutes consent to a given act, because he gets into this *It Was My Fault* mindset sometimes and needs to find his way out of that thought tunnel. I have tried telling him it wasn't his fault, but he's a teenager, he doesn't listen to me.

One specific question that came up was 'When is it rape?' A lot of states have gotten away from using the word 'rape', instead preferring to use phrases like 'unlawful sexual conduct' or 'sexual assault', but the legal definition of rape used by the Department of Justice is *Penetration, no matter how slight, of the vagina or anus with any body part or object, or oral penetration by a sex organ of another person, without the consent of the victim.* Updates to the law state that all genders can be victimized and also include the idea that 'object rape'—penetration using an object rather than a sex organ—also applies.

Somewhere in our late-night legal literature review we came across a notation saying that there was no duration requirement required for an act to constitute rape. We spotted this piece of information, looked at each other with a sort of sick shock, and the same completely insane thought landed in both our brains at exactly the same time, and that thought was, "Duration??!!"

Among our questions: Are you supposed to be watching a clock while getting raped? How about a stopwatch, should you carry one of those around just in case you need it, along with your pepper spray and personal alarm? Do you say, "Hold on, rapist person, I just need to reset this to zero, and you should know that in fifteen seconds you'll be guilty of a felony." If you don't have a stopwatch, is it acceptable to count, "One Mississippi, two Mississippi..." and if so is that information admissible in court? Why is it always Mississippi? Other states have four syllable names too. Nobody ever counts, "One Colorado, two Colorado…" What if you lose count? What if all you have available is a sundial? What degree of precision is required for evidence purposes; do we need tenths of seconds, or hundredths of seconds, or what?

This whole series of ideas, besides being incredibly sick, also struck both of us as uproariously hilarious. We could. Not. Stop. We would sort of get calmed down and then one of us would go, "One Mississippi…" and we'd be off again.

This phenomenon is a common refrain in our late-night conversations. We hang out together and talk about how this sucks or that sucks and I listen while he processes some of the pain, and then somebody says something really dumb and we laugh our idiot selves silly, and then finally he can get to sleep, which means so can I.

Jayce: Why Is This Shit Funny?

Before I became a Price, I was constantly in survival mode. Every day was a battle and I often had no idea how I was to push through to the next day. I was quiet. I was closed off. I lived mostly on my phone and would lose myself in music. Those things helped, but the most important defense and survival mechanism I developed was humor. As things got worse in my old house and it was either laugh or cry, I chose to learn to laugh at myself and find the laughable moments in the worst situations.

Now my sense of humor is one of the things I'm most proud of, because it's literally saved me on multiple occasions. It's healthier than coping mechanisms like cutting or substance abuse, and I'm happier with myself because now I know I wasn't naturally shy. I'm naturally goofy, and I'm happy that that is a part of who I am.

Laughter still gets me through the toughest circumstances and it's safe to say that I would not be myself if I couldn't find the funny things in my life.

Chapter 14
Kelly: Mindfulness For The Teenaged Brain

Our Kaiden is a super smart kid who is also prone to major depression and serious anxiety. He's ridden the Psychotherapy Train past Self Esteem Lowlands and through the Chasm of Perfectionism himself, and more than once he's ended up on a little circular spur of stupidity that goes, "I suck, so I won't do my homework, because if I do I'll just do it wrong, because I suck..." and eventually a railroad crew comprised of family, clinicians, and some drugs blows up the spur and lays new, straighter track leading to the Castle of Self Actualization in the Land of Sanity.

Now, if you have any experience with therapeutic interventions, you have very probably come across a lot of bullshit. I am in no way disparaging people who get relief from—or practice—alternative therapies, but I am prone to rolling my eyes so loud you can hear it in the next room when I am faced with anything that involves crystals, unregulated herbs, astral travel, or anything nebulously called 'energy work.' I do not believe marijuana cures everything. I live in Colorado, where this statement is seen as sacrilege, but I'm sticking to my guns here and until I see some peer reviewed studies saying that CBD oil really DOES cause amputated body parts to grow back. If you tell me this I will assume you are just blowing smoke up my ass. Literally.

Still, I have seen weird enough things in 29 years of nursing practice to cause me to think twice before dismissing anything a patient says works, because first of all, if it works, my job just got easier *and I didn't have to do any work*, and second, there are more things in heaven and on Earth than are dreamt of in my philosophy, even though I am not called Horatio.

One very common recommendation given to those of us who seem to be intractable in terms of giving up our pathological neuroses is meditation, or rather the Bud Light to meditation's Guinness: Mindfulness. To do mindfulness you are supposed to spend time looking at what is going on around you and maintaining your sensory connection to the present time, while at the same time not placing any type of value judgements on your feelings or your body's response to those feelings. Mindfulness exercises involve doing sensory things that command your attention so you can no longer perseverate on why you keep dating people with the emotional intelligence of amoebas and why eating your feelings has to taste so damn good.

When you call the crisis hotline in the middle of the night, their goal is to keep you alive and out of the actual emergency room, so they tend to suggest doing some of these exercises, either alone or with a supportive somebody else who is willing to act as Sancho to your crazy-ass Don Quixote. They'll say things like, "Listen to soothing music, or look at something beautiful, or smell a lovely flower…" You get my drift. Then they throw a lot of research your way that proves that if you'll only do this stuff, no more windmills will have to die, and you go off in a state that if not precisely hopeful is at least conciliatory with your own mind.

Unless, that is, you're a teenager.

Teenagers are transcending the magical thinking of their childhoods, where unicorns and fairness exist and corporations are not people, and beginning to stare into the void of their own pointlessness and the potential banality of their own future lives. It is the first time in life when a person asks, "Is this all there is? Where's my unicorn? What the hell is FICA and why am I giving them so much money?"

This means that developmentally speaking, the teenage brain is absolutely primed for the installation of an app called Sarcasm. The app connects seamlessly to a teenager's communication and logic circuits and acts to help the user interface with the cruelty and indifference of the world in a way that prevents all the user's data from being erased. It's a learning app too. It assesses the teenager's level of sophistication, experience, and jadedness and produces tailored messages on a spectrum ranging from Tween to Liberal Arts College Philosophy Major With A Trust Fund.

Imagine, if you will, a tween being bullied at school for something superficial like whether or not her mascara looks like spiders are date-raping her eyeballs. "God," the bully will say, "Your mascara. Is so… spiderish." Now, the tween can deploy the Sarcasm app and respond at the Tween level, which will result in something like, "At least I *wear* mascara." As comebacks go it leaves a bit to be desired. It lacks zing, sophistication, and style. It leaves you unsatisfied when you're told the story, in an 'I guess you had to be there' kind of way.

The same kid three years later will have a more panoramic worldview and will be able to come back with something like "At least I don't steal my mascara from my uncle's funeral home." This packs a bit more punch, it's a little edgier, more satisfying. There's death, and some darkness, and a mysterious uncle in a dark suit who is good with cosmetics.

Fast forward to college and all of a sudden the app can put out communiques that make absolutely no sense whatsoever but that somehow make you feel like when you hear them *you* are the dumb one for not understanding all the subtle ramifications of the statement. "At least I'm not gazing into an abyss, because if you gaze too long into an abyss, the abyss gazes also into you. – Nietzsche." The listener suspects this is bullshit, but is just uncertain enough to wonder if they've completely comprehended all the nuances of the statement and to question whether they are as smart as they thought they were.

Such people cannot be sold the bill of goods that is 'go smell a pretty flower' as a treatment for their anxiety and depression. They are not buying. They believe that pretty flowers mask existential pain. They believe that the person prescribing this to them as a remedy is either a Teletubby or an idiot.

Which brings us to the question of what the hell to actually do with them when we are faced with the parental task of building a bridge to the goal of peaceful sanity over the barrier of teenage jadedness.

The answer is to tailor mindfulness activities in ways that connect well with the teenage mind. The secret ingredient: absolute bullshit.

One prime example of this is a guided meditation currently available on YouTube called *Fuck That*. You're presented with a bucolic ocean scene with waves gently breaking over a sun-kissed, lovely beach positively bursting with perfectly formed seashells and no rotting whale carcasses or sand fleas within a thousand miles. The guy who narrates the thing's name is Jason Headley and he has a voice you would believe no matter what he said, and he delivers his monologue in this soothing murmur that allows you to sort of drift off into serenity like you're undergoing light anesthesia. "Just let allllllllllll that bullshit faaaaaaaade away. Fuuuuuuuccckkk thaaaaaaat."

My teenagers LOVE this little four-minute piece of claptrap, and damned if it hasn't actually proven to be quite effective as a calming exercise. One, because if you actually try to participate in the meditation part of it you DO get relaxed, and two, because if something is funny and you laugh, you get a lot of physiological benefits from that as well. Laughter has been shown to decrease stress hormones, increase your immune responses, and promote a generally relaxed sort of well-being. This explains why Jayce is rarely sick, the kid laughs all the time.

One night when he was feeling especially anxious and anticipating a bunch of flashbacks of an anniversary nature, I made him a list of teen-friendly mindfulness and grounding exercises to try. I was feeling especially ingenious and parentally cocky as I did this, because I was convinced that if he actually did the things on the list he would feel a lot better. Usually when you feel ingenious and cocky the world is about to smite you hard and put you in your place, and this night was no exception, but I was being Proactive and Promoting Independence and allowing Jayce to be Self- Empowering.

"Jayce. I want you to try some stuff tonight."

"Oh shit, really? I don't wanna," he said.

"Yes, here is a Plan. I have created a Plan for you to use if you get to feeling awful. Look, it is on paper."

That, of course, was Mistake #1, because teenagers only want to pay attention to stuff if it's on a screen. This flat white wood pulp you can write on holds no magic for them.

"Dude. Put the phone down and look at this."

His eyes s-l-o-w-l-y dragged themselves away from the screen and he sighed at me.

"I don't need a plan. I am gonna wing it."

He has learned by now that when I get a bee in my hat about something I am not going away until he gives me his actual attention, though, so he made another of those inarticulate noises at me that translated into "Oh fuck, just tell me what your plan is, Mom, you're going to anyway". So I did.

"I want you to work your way down this list and choose some of these things to do to bring you back to the here and now," I told him. The list in question included *Fuck That*, creating a playlist of songs that felt uplifting or empowering (which back in my day would have included Twisted Sister's *We're Not Gonna Take It*), writing stories or drawing art, and doing some breathing or yoga exercises.

I pestered him until he agreed that some of these things sounded like a good idea, and then he got sort of engaged with the whole project and made his uplifting and empowering playlist, did one of the writing things, and drew a sketch of Mari that was actually pretty good, and seeing him thus involved in his own self-preservation, I went to bed. Whereupon an hour and a half later, right as the dream sequence where Ben and Jerry run me through the enrober machine and coat me in creamy dark chocolaty goodness was beginning, he came in my room in full Jaycequake mode and I traipsed back downstairs, ruefully contemplating raiding his Halloween candy bag as soon as he fell asleep. Whether or not I actually DID this heinous thing is something I will let the reader conjecture about, because by now you've got a reasonable picture of my overall character. Of course I did.

Jayce: Minding Mindfulness Majorly

Usually when I think of mindfulness, I think of doing yoga, sitting there going "Ommmmm… My legs are killing meeeee…." Meditation has never worked for me, because I can't sit still to save my life. My version of mindfulness is active. I go for a walk, and that's the time when I can just think. That's also when most of my songs get written.

If I actually do have to sit there and meditate, I love the *Fuck That* video. That guy's voice is just so calming. Now it's funny because I had a whole lesson in my college psych class where my professor played that video and we all learned to say "Fuck it…" I took notes and sent the link to Anna because she was studying for a whole bunch of AP exams and I thought she could also use a lesson on letting go of bullshit. Once in a while I pick another group of friends and send it to them, saying "I think this really fits your life right now."

What calms me the most is listening to music that is either entertaining or that gets me thinking about things I otherwise wouldn't. My dad sent me a YouTube video by this British guy named Thomas Benjamin Wild, Esq. The song is called "I've No More Fucks To Give" and the guy is manhandling a ukulele in a men's clothing store and having a grand old time.

Screw meditation, screw sitting cross-legged, just hold up your middle fingers and say, "Fuck that."

143

Chapter 15

Kelly: A Series Of Unfortunate Events

"Hello, Colorado Crisis Center, this is [Jayce's deadname] speaking, how can I help you?" Jayce had gone over the edge of control again and some sort of intervention was gonna be a thing, and it was sort of up in the air whether it would be this or a 911 call. It was seriously snowy and the roads were dreadful, so me driving him to the clinic wasn't going to happen.

"Oh God," I said, looking down at the terrified child shaking in my lap and thinking well, you REALLY cannot make this shit up. "Um. Hi. I don't think you CAN help me, actually." Jayce was making sort of inarticulate freaking-out noises on the floor at the top of the stairs. I was trying to be a steadying influence while on the phone with the crisis line so he could talk to a clinician.

"I'm sure there's something we can talk over for you," she said, totally not understanding. I couldn't blame her for this, because she really was lacking a whole bunch of salient facts. I didn't want to discuss these facts with her while Jayce was in his semi-sentient panic state next to me, because he was almost as triggered by hearing his deadname as he was by whatever circumstance had sent him into this state in the first place. It didn't seem like a course of action calculated to make things better.

"No, that wasn't what I meant, see, I am calling on behalf of my son, who is feeling miserable and suicidal tonight. You could help him, except there's a problem. Can I just talk to somebody else?"

By now the counselor was thoroughly confused, but she'd been well trained and she's kind and she said, "Okay. Can you tell me something about why you'd like to speak to a different clinician?"

I gave her Jayce's name so she could get to his chart. "Can you see Jayce's legal name?" I asked her.

"No..."

"You have the same name."

Jayce at this point had figured out what was happening on the other end of the phone and made a noise like a very irritated muskrat being thrown into a wall. Said noise was meant to indicate that for him, talking to a crisis counselor who shared his deadname was simply not going to be effective in any way and that he would therefore rather just suffer, if it was all the same to me.

"I'm sorry, I'm confused," she said.

"Your name. Jayce is transgender, and your name is the same as his former name. His deadname, which he never, ever uses, and finds pretty triggering."

"Oh!! I get it now. Okay, you just call back, the odds are good you'll get somebody else. Thanks for clearing it up for me."

The next counselor was a guy named Tim. That worked a little better, although in my unhinged exhausted state I kept thinking of him as Tim the Enchanter the entire time. In my brain, John Cleese was wearing this weird costume that had ram horns and shooting little explosions all over the place intoning, "Cave of Caerbannog Crisis Center, how can I help you?" and me going, "I'm pretty sure the Vorpal Bunny has control of my transgender son's brain…"

The crisis from the beginning of this chapter escalated over the next couple of weeks and then things finally got scary enough for me to feel like we couldn't keep Jayce safe at his current level of care and so one morning after a particularly harrowing night I said, "Dude. We need to think about getting you an inpatient hospital stay."

This idea was met with immediate and decisive protest of the 'Mom. No. I gotta go to work' variety, which I found sort of ruefully amusing since if one is imminently suicidal 'work' is kinda near the bottom of the priority list. The boy was not in a mental frame of mind that would allow him to be alone, and since having your mom follow you all around your job site at work going, "Okay, you can use the pen, but only if you don't use it to self-harm" decreases your professional confidence, I sort of snorted at him and said, "Jayce. You cannot possibly go to work. You cannot go anywhere. You don't get to drive. You're flat out not safe just now, kiddo."

This was most assuredly not a decision I made lightly. Kaiden was hospitalized at the age of 11 for similar issues and the experience was dreadful. Terrifying, lonely, and overwhelming for all of us. While they were there, a nurse practitioner who disliked me intensely for questioning her clinical judgement actually falsified information on Kaiden's chart, causing me to go completely ballistic and involve the hospital's patient advocacy department, the Department of Regulatory Agencies, and Joint Commission. It was seriously bad and I have approached almost all versions of psychiatric care with a cynical and wary trepidation ever since then, especially where my kids are concerned.

Eventually I wore Jayce down and we set off for the little emergency department at a local hospital to discuss a treatment plan for escalated suicide risk. They did an assessment and decided that yes, he definitely needed to be admitted, and they offered him the option to voluntarily sign himself in. They got an A+ from Mama Bear over here because they handled the transgender thing beautifully. They just said okay, you won't have a roommate, how's that? And then they were very, very good about only calling him Jayce throughout the whole five day stay. I delivered a short lecture about working the program and taking advantage of what they had to offer, promised to deliver some clothes later that day, hugged him hard, left, and had a good cry in the parking lot.

Because he is who he is, he flung himself into the treatment with a will. He went to every single group. He played basketball, talked to people, did art therapy, attended the entire caboodle of options that were available to him, and even made friends. And dammit, he paid attention and he learned stuff in there. He developed his own safety plan, learned some things about self-evaluation, and got started on a parent (me) -approved medication that was really helpful right from the beginning. It was like an educational sort of summer camp experience with a lot of other suicidal people. This idea got me thinking about what camp songs might be sung there at night by the campfire. I pictured a bearded psychiatrist with an Austrian accent and a guitar strumming singalong tunes with titles like *If You're Happy And You Know It (Why Are You Here?)* and *Make New Friends, But Don't Enable Or Invalidate Them*. Everyone would toast a marshmallow, then add a piece of chocolate, some graham crackers, and their evening medication. The result would be a delightful camp dessert guaranteed to inspire feelings of tranquility and promote restful sleep.

We never missed a visiting hour, and believe it or not, we usually had fun. Visiting time was held in the cafeteria. People would go to see someone who was a patient in the facility, sit down across a table with them, say a few words and then mostly sit silently until the time was up. On the other hand, we tended to be loud and happy to see one another, and we seemed to have these pressurized stores of goofiness that needed to escape. The day room had this big chalk wall in it where people were supposed to write inspirational messages like *You Are Enough* and

Every Cloud Has A Silver Lining and such. I thought for a minute and then wrote *Everything Is Funny... Eventually.*"

One of our more warped creative endeavors while he was in there involved the Seven Dwarfs of the Psych Hospital. Their names, we decided over styrofoam cups of soda in the hospital cafeteria, were Sedated, Delusional, High, Triggered, Catatonic, Batshit, and Flight Risk. Jayce has drawn little cartoons of most of these, but owing to their resemblance to Disney characters we really cannot share. Around this same time, Jayce's bestie, Anna, had managed to fall on her head during a dance class and give herself a concussion, and for her we developed the Seven Dwarfs of Head Injury: Sleepy, Grumpy, Dopey, Teary, Impulsive, Ouchy, and Confused. I told her the expected rate of recovery was about half a dwarf a week, thus helping clear up the whole question of 'Why Do I Feel Like This And When Will It Stop?'

I also called the hospital a lot, which caused both Jayce and the nurses to think I was slightly nuts. This became part of my daily routine when Kaiden was a baby and was in the neonatal intensive care unit. I would spend every day there with him for twelve hours, then go home. We'd call before going to bed, I called in the middle of the night when I got up to pump milk for them, then we called again about 5:00 am and then Daniel would go see him before he went to work. We did this for four months straight. When there's a Price kid in the hospital, it's just normal for us to be in this sort of continual contact that the nursing staff generally find annoying as hell.

"Mom. Did you really call the nurse's station at 5:45 this morning?"

"I really did. I told you I would." (Apparently he hadn't believed me when I told him this.)

"What did they tell you?" he wondered.

"Well, mostly that you'd been asleep since they came on shift and to call back when you were awake." (I did this, too.)

He would shake his head in bemused wonder at the idea that somebody could be enough of a helicopter lunatic parent to need to call and find out if he got any sleep at 5:45 every morning. I shook MY head in bemused wonder that he didn't know this.

He came out of there considerably stronger and more grounded, with some new closure on his family history and some new tools. He said it was one of the most beneficial things he'd ever done for himself. Personally, I think it would have been slightly better with Seroquel S'mores, but that's just me.

Jayce: I Can't Go To The Hospital, I Have Work

If I remember correctly, I was in shaky panic attack mode again and as usual I was resisting any intervention. I just kept saying "I'm fine, leave me the hell alone." I was at the top of the stairs debating whether to just fall down the stairs and possibly crack my head open, so I was utterly failing to convince my mom that I was okay.

She insisted on calling the crisis center and got the clinician who shared my deadname. I heard her pleading with this lady about how we needed a different counselor and I eventually figured out what the problem was. It wasn't funny in the slightest at the time, but later on it definitely was. The second clinician, Tim, was able to talk me down for the night. I thought once that was over, I was fine but that call was actually the beginning of a downward spiral that led me into the hospital.

I didn't really realize I was in such a dangerous and self-destructive state of mind, and one afternoon I went to visit Anna. She had recently fallen off some aerial equipment at dance class and so I wanted to go see her and take her some candy. She'd done that for me once before and I wanted to reciprocate.

That morning I had woken up at like 6:30 and had done some self-harm damage to my arms, but later on I went to Anna's house and it seemed like a pretty normal visit. We were laughing and giving each other crap like we always did, but I was carrying something dangerous with me at the time and I had a plan to take my own life. It wasn't outwardly obvious, but I was in serious trouble. I wasn't looking for someone to save me that day, but I was standing there talking and laughing with her and I started to feel like I wanted more of those moments, so I pulled her aside and said, "I think I need help."

She said "Thank you for telling me. You realize there is no way in hell you are leaving my house with a dangerous item in your possession, so give it to me now and I will be talking to your mom."

"Totally fair, thank you," I said and drove home.

Shortly afterward my mom got a cheery text from Anna that

said "Good afternoon. I just want you to know that Jayce came to me this afternoon with something dangerous on him. He gave it to me but I think he's in trouble."

Mom responded to this with "Well great! The festivities this evening will now include getting him some help and going through his room!"

The next day I ended up at the hospital. At first, I felt like a deer in the headlights. I had no idea what to expect but I had definitely heard a lot of horror stories from my friends who had previously been through psych hospital stays, and adding the transgender factor made it even scarier because I didn't know how they would handle it. I didn't think they would be respectful or accommodating, but they were actually terrific. They were really good about my name and pronouns, and they allowed me to have my own room because I was uncomfortable sharing with anyone at that time.

I was pretty quiet the first few hours because I felt kind of bewildered, but I ended up in a 'processing' group and it turned out I had a hell of a lot of stuff to process. I met a person in that group who is still a friend. They were kind and made me feel a whole lot more at ease by telling me stories about their spider encounters in Australia. I decided right then that I was never, ever going to Australia.

That was kind of the icebreaker, and afterward I found there were more people to talk to and even have some fun with. I actually had fun at the psych hospital. I played basketball, did art therapy, and started to talk about and deal with things from my past. I came out of the hospital not feeling so ashamed of those things, especially since there were a lot of people there who had had similar experiences. It was one of the most beneficial things I had ever done for myself, and it was exactly what I needed at that time to get me back on track.

Chapter 16

Kelly: Sex, Seroquel, and Beer

After the hospital stay it became obviously imperative that we take some steps around the house to keep Jayce as safe as possible, and so one of the things we did was lock up all the drugs in the house in a fire safe. I kept the only key, which as of this writing I have not yet lost. I left out the laxatives, because that seemed like an unlikely way for someone to try to kill themselves, but there was still not enough room in the stupid box for all the medications everybody took. Fitting them all in there became a demented Tetris game that involved cursing a lot and repeatedly taking things out, rearranging them, and putting them back in.

One day I was trying to fit all the meds into the damn box – again – after giving Gabi her morning stuff, and suddenly a thought hit me about a way to make some room in there that was absolutely not going to be a problem for Jayce, and I started to laugh like a hyena. The fire safe is kept on Daniel's closet floor, and let me tell you, giggling aloud while alone in a closet with a handful of drugs is not a parenting experience that is discussed in any of the books. It had dawned on me suddenly that it would be perfectly safe to take Kaiden's birth control pills out of there and put them pretty much anyplace at all because there was no force on Earth that was going to make my transgender boy try to OD on estrogen. (Kaiden was on birth control for menstrual suppression at the time, because guys don't like periods..) Of course, I immediately had to text this to Jayce, because of the Black Sense of Humor thing alluded to heavily in a previous chapter, and he also found it funny as hell.

As is often the case around here, the dementia increased and it became necessary for me to write a very bad country western song on the subject. (Jayce thought he'd amend the lyrics after I wrote the thing, but here is my original version, complete and intact.)

The Estrogen Song

We lock up all the drugs here, we have to, don't you see.
Our kids need love and safety, and the oldest one's a 'he',
He's macho and he's manly, and that's the reason why,

It's safe to leave out the estrogen.

The painkillers and Pepto, the Adderall and such,
The serotonin boosters, any one could be too much,
So we're cautious and we're careful,
there's no room left in the box

But it's safe to leave out the estrogen.

(Bridge!)

For our boy'd give up at least three limbs before he'd be portrayed
As anything remotely female. This is why we're unafraid
Of leaving pill packs scattered everywhere, the bed, the couch, the floor

Just as long as they all contain estrogen.

We could leave all the drugs lying out in the open, throw caution right out to
the wind
If the drug makers put 'em in pink-colored plastic, like the wardrobe of
Barbie's best friend,
Print the pill packs with all of the days of the week, put exactly four weeks
in a pack,
Then this boy wouldn't touch 'em, he'd leave them alone, walk away and not
ever look back

'Cause they'd all look exactly like estrogen.

See you at the Grammys.

There comes a time in the life of every young man when he starts thinking thoughts about debauchery of various types. The urge to sow one's wild oats, see the seedier side of life, and generally go have experiences that aren't the sort to tell your mom about comes upon them. They develop this sort of constant leer in their expression, and while they may not be leering at any actual living human they find attractive, the odds are good that they're leering at someone in their imaginations. They get restless and having to clean up the kitchen feels dreadfully confining. Most kids in late adolescence end up with some stories that they swear they will never tell their own kids when they have some.

Jayce is no exception. He, too, would enjoy the opportunity to engage in some irresponsible but entertaining behavior. He's limited by the language in The Contract, however, and things like overnight guests and the use of mind-altering substances are prohibited. This is partially because I do not want to spend time explaining to the younger kids in the house why there's a girl nobody knows sleeping in their brother's room. Revolving doors through which sexy strangers pass are just not going to be a thing here. I am not running a brothel, a frat house, or a bachelor pad. (When Jayce reads this he will say, "Aww...") I also cannot risk setting up a standard that would allow my other teenager to decide that what the hell, he'd like a little action too. Down that path madness lies.

Being transgender presents some challenges in the dating arena, for reasons that are probably fairly obvious and that can be broken down into two different sections of romantic life about which I feel the need to make a terrible double entendre here: In and Out. Either the person you are dating knows you are transgender, because you are Out of the proverbial closet, or they don't, which means you are In. The decision about when—or if—to disclose this information is a complicated one for sure, with thousands of different variables to consider including how open minded your date is, where you met them and who introduced you, and how motivated you are to get to the disclosure point based on a totally arbitrary mathematical construct I will call the inhibition/desperation/hotness relationship (IDHR.)

For the purposes of this book, since Jayce is straight, I will go ahead and use female gender pronouns for all of his many girlfriends. Imagine that you are eighteen years old, unequivocally male, and that you have a date planned for a given Friday night. If your date is already aware that you are trans, your inhibition number goes down because you don't have to closely guard that fact. If she is unaware, your inhibition number goes up. The inhibition factor is tempered by the Variable of Enthusiasm, which is the young lady's response to your being transgender and which may vary from 'Holy crap, swipe right' down through 'Meh' and into 'Oh hell no'. Call this I to the power of VE, or I^{VE}. Now put the desperation piece into the puzzle; how long has it been since you had an actual date or relationship, and how do you feel about that? If you are a typical eighteen-year-old male and it's been a while, where 'a while' could mean anything from a few minutes to forever, your desperation number will be someplace in the 'Code Red, Gonna Die' area. I don't think most guys this age ever drop much below Code Red, so we will call this number the Desperation Constant. Since red light has an average wavelength of 667.5 nanometers, we will use this number for the Desperation Constant just for the hell of it. Next, we can look at the variable of Hotness, which is on a Scoville scale with Emma Watson at the top (3.3 million Scoville units, arbitrarily) and which descends from there and is influenced heavily by the Stephen Stills Exponent of Attainability (SEA) (Because of *Love The One You're With*, for you whippersnappers in the crowd.) Our formula, therefore, is as follows:

$$DC * h^{SEA} / I^{VE} = IDHR$$

By way of example we will revisit the case of Emma Watson. If the Desperation Constant is 667.5, hotness is 3.3 million Scoville units, with a Stills Attainability value of -7 and she has no idea of the trans status of the stud in question (I=2) but you know she would be openminded (VE=5) because she said so on Twitter, this gives us an absolute bullshit value for IHDR as follows:

$$IHDR = 667.5 * 3,300,000^{-7} / 2^5 = -68,835,791.48$$

The lesson here, besides 'man, there are a lot of really dumb uses for math' is that a negative number that big means it's a good thing Emma Watson is not the only woman on Earth.

Jayce recently started on injectable testosterone. This means that once a week he voluntarily takes a drug that increases his desire to perpetrate indecent acts. Having never raised a boy through puberty, I admit to a little trepidation about this prospect. I suspect the most effective strategy will be to maintain a sense of humor, which fortunately is a talent I possess, and also provide a hell of a lot of very openminded education. Emma Watson, at least an imaginary version of her, is very likely here to stay. Thanks, Emma.

The transgender community, like the disabled community, is woefully underserved when it comes to sexual health services. There's this tendency in society to look at somebody who is trans or somebody with a disability and just decide they'll figure it out— if they even need to worry about it at all. There's also a tendency for potential dating partners to immediately jump to the question of anatomy when considering dating a transgender person.

My personal philosophy on this subject (from my lofty, privileged, cisgender perch) is that anatomy is superseded by more cerebral aspects of sexuality for these kids. Inserting tab A into slot B is simply not all there is to it, nor should it be. Communication, creativity, humor (again!) and imagination are tools that are useful for any healthy sex life.

When I was a teenager my personal heroine was Dr. Ruth Westheimer, who showed up on radio stations nationwide once a week exhorting people to have "GOOT sex!" in her thick German accent. She was everybody's sweet grandma and she would tell you in no uncertain terms that you not only could get laid a lot, you *should*, albeit safely and with appropriate consent and communication. She advocated for female orgasms, masturbation, role playing, and all kinds of other things at a time when they were thoroughly taboo, and she did it in this refreshingly direct way that made people wonder why the hell the topic had been off limits in the first place. I listened to her radio show religiously.

In high school in the mid-eighties I had something of a reputation as an early public health nurse. At age fifteen I was known as the girl who would visit the local grocery store and buy people contraceptives. Condoms, foams, sponges, you name it, I would go get it. People would slip notes and cash into my locker with specific requests and I would stroll in there and decimate the shelves. Before big weekends like Homecoming I would sometimes have a couple of hundred dollars' worth of requests. If people didn't know how to use something I would either explain or demonstrate (using a banana, so get your minds out of the gutter).

By age sixteen, when I could drive, I took multiple people to the local county public health clinic for birth control pills, STD testing, and exams. The nurse practitioners there knew me very well. The clinic charged for services on a sliding scale that generally came down to 'What can you afford to pay today?' They would also treat people using false names and agree to phone results of tests and such over to my house, since HIPAA wasn't a thing yet and patient confidentiality was a totally foreign concept. This caused my father occasional consternation when he'd answer the phone and be informed by a kindly voice on the other phone that somebody he didn't know had chlamydia and needed to go pick up an antibiotic prescription.

The upshot of all this reminiscing is that I am and always have been completely matter-of-fact about sex.

Jayce has taken to asking me questions like, "When will you all be out of the house while I have a girl over here?" as though this is something I will just block out space for in my calendar. Like, "*Tuesday: Dentist. Thursday: Quality Girl Time for Jayce. Friday: PTA meeting*". He is sad to learn that some things just have to be spontaneous and occur when they work out. He's also at least moderately motivated to find a girlfriend with her own apartment. If you know anybody, message him.

The legal drinking age in Colorado is 21. Marijuana is also legal here for recreational use, causing Colorado Girl Scouts to rejoice when they are given an annual opportunity to sell cookies outside the pot shops. (Yes, this is real. Yes, they do sell a lot of cookies there.)

A recent conversation on this subject went like this:

"Mom. When I turn 21 if I want to have a drink, you can't stop me."

"Jayce. You cannot mix alcohol and psych meds."

We (okay me) came to an agreement on a plan for this. If he truly needs to feel like a typical 21-year-old boy on that date, he can take an extra Seroquel and dump a beer over his head.

Wish me luck.

Jayce: Stuff That Would Get me Grounded

If you're reading this book, and if for some reason you still don't think I'm a typical teenage boy, this chapter will probably – and hopefully – change your opinion on that. I consider myself a very typical teenage boy. Here are some examples: I get quite excited when my mom tells me I'm a slob and I have the tendency to want to bring girls home when no one else is there, (although none of the ones I pick actually want to come back with me).

A major change that happens to boys on testosterone, and I'm sorry for all the mothers out there, is this: If you have a transgender son, and that son is not necessarily interested in sex and doesn't seem to have much of a sex drive, when you throw that kid on testosterone that is likely to change very quickly. So consider yourself warned and be prepared for that.

One thing that is very misunderstood and disrespected when it comes to trans kids is the idea that trans kids have the right to a healthy sex life just the same as cisgender kids do. There is not a whole lot of education out there about transgender people having healthy, normalized sex lives. A lot of trans people think things like: "No one is going to want to get involved with me," and" I'm a freak," and "there's something wrong with my body because it doesn't match or I've had surgical modifications," or whatever. That is one thing that was told to me by my former mother, the idea that I am going to be depriving some girl of a sexual experience with a "real guy." It got to me for a while, but it turns out that is crap.

Like my mom wrote in the book, it's really not about anatomy or how a person is born. Your greatest asset for sexual activity is your brain. That's where the fun and creativity and spontaneity come from. Worrying about your anatomy is really pointless, because believe it or not a lot of people out there are going to be generally open-minded. Whoever my partner is, they're going to need to understand that I'm trans and I have trauma. For me and pretty much every other trans person out there, that's going to need to be something that's entirely acceptable.

From my experience, when you're trans, dating is terrifying. Connecting with people romantically is already hard and then adding being trans on top of it just makes it worse. In the game room at school I would always hear all these bullshit stories from guys about how hooking up with people is so easy and just naturally happens and the girls just come to them. You ask out an incredibly hot girl and she goes out with you and then you end up married and that's all there is to it. It's absolute crap.

It doesn't help that at that time I was absolutely clueless about whether or not someone was flirting with me. In the winter of 2018, I attended a Greyson Chance concert in Denver. My date for the evening was my mom. The concert was at this dive bar in Denver and Mom decided it was a bad idea to send her trans kid to a dive bar alone, so off we went. We had meet and greet tickets, and after the show we were standing around waiting to meet Greyson. My mom stepped out to use the restroom and I got to talking to a group of girls. I was especially connecting with a girl named Rachel. She was cute and nice and she scored major points with my mom by asking her if she was my sister. We kept talking, and then we got to meet Greyson (when my mom introduced herself to him, she said, "Hi Greyson, my name is Mom" and he said "Oh whoops, sorry about all the cursing…") and then we left.

As we were walking to the car my mom said to me "Hey, doofus, when a cute girl talks to you, you're supposed to get her number."

"She didn't like me," I said.

"Yes, she definitely did," said my mom, and so I was kicking myself for not getting her number.

The next day I decided to try to get in contact with her again. I knew her name, her age, and what college she went to. I also knew she followed Greyson on Instagram, which was how she knew about the VIP meet and greet. So, I searched for her name under his followers, messaged her, and said "Hey, I was stupid last night," and got her number.

Unfortunately, she has a boyfriend now.

It's so scary because I've had experiences that weren't that positive. The first date I had after starting college was with a girl who knew I was trans and took the opportunity to ask a lot of really invasive, personal questions about my sex life. She liked me and I liked her but her parents weren't okay with it so we just stayed friends.

When I did get my first girlfriend, it took me maybe two weeks to even talk to her, let alone ask her out. I would start talking to her in class or the game room, then let her go on about her day, and I still had no phone number, no social media info, no contact of any kind. Finally, I got to the point where I let her walk away again and I said to myself "Hey, dumbass, what are you gonna do about this?"

I eventually got the chance to walk her to her car, got her number, and said "Oh, by the way, would you be interested in going out with me?" It blew my mind when she said yes. That was the biggest dating accomplishment I've had, and I'm what, 20?

So we went out and I hadn't told her yet that I was trans. I thought everyone at school just knew, I don't exactly hide it there, but apparently she didn't know. I told her and her mouth dropped open and she said, "Okay wait, you were born female?" And then she was like "Oh, well that's cool." We ended up breaking up when the pandemic hit because we were headed down different paths and couldn't see each other, but we're still friends.

There have been a few other people I've asked out with mixed results. I have now figured out that if I want people to go out with me, I have to actually ask them. My desperation constant is now well above my mom's silly 667.5 number. I'm at the point now where I don't even need a girlfriend, I just need a girl. I'm open to all kinds of girls, trans, cis, doesn't matter. If you're female and cute, I'd just like a few hours of your time.

I've also never been one to get involved in underage drinking, or smoking, or substance abuse of any kind. Although I was encouraged to do that in my former household, I never got into the habit, never became much of a drinker or smoker. Now that I'm about to turn 21 the thought has occurred to me that it would be fun to walk through the house with a six pack of beer just because I can. If I did, I wouldn't be a good example to my siblings, and it's also been brought to my clear attention that it's not a good idea to mix alcohol with psych medication. Sure, it's probably okay to have one drink, in moderation, and be safe and don't drive, and feel like you're a big deal because you're 21 and have alcohol in one hand. In my case, if I feel the need to participate in a social situation I'll just hold the beer in one hand and my Seroquel in the other. What else could you possibly need?

Chapter 17

Kelly: Remodeling The Boy

In early March of 2019 I took Jayce back to Children's TRUE Clinic for Gender Diversity in Aurora to discuss the next part of the transition plan and talk with them about getting him onto hormones. If you're a trans guy, you have a few different options for providing yourself with induced manhood, and these include intramuscular injections, subcutaneous injections, and transdermal skin patches. Most guys start out with the injectable form of the drug. Some stay on that form forever, others might switch to the skin patches once their levels stabilize, it's all dependent on what they and their clinicians decide makes the most sense.

For Jayce, the approach the team chose was the subcutaneous injections. Once a week he gives himself a shot of testosterone in the subcutaneous tissue on his stomach. There's a learning curve involved when starting T, though, because you have to draw the right dose of the drug up in your syringe with one needle, then change needles without contaminating anything or stabbing yourself (or your mom), then correctly inject the drug into the right place on your body.

That first day at the TRUE clinic they took him back, ran a bunch of tests, and told him he could start on hormone therapy that day if he wanted to. "Cool!" I said excitedly, "Can I come with you?"

"No!" he said in this aggrieved 'God, Mom, what the hell did you just ask me, I am so embarrassed,' teenager tone.

Okay, fine.

So I was left alone in the waiting room with nothing good to read and rapidly dwindling phone battery power, and while sitting there I got to bitching about the fact that I was sitting there alone missing this major turning point in my boy's life with Anna's mom, Michelle.

"This sucks," I grouched over Facebook. "The kid won't let me go record his milestone moment. Waaah. He is being mean to me."

Michelle is one of those naturally proactive people who Gets Crap Done, and she is also a professional photographer who has recorded her children's lives in exhaustive detail with the kinds of cameras that weigh fifteen pounds and have all kinds of attachments you have to change to get the right effects. Imagine my gratitude when she took it upon herself to get on Jayce's case via smartphone.

"If it was my kid doing this I'd be over there with my Nikon, you understand," she told him. "Do not make me come over there."

I was therefore surprised and delighted when a few minutes later Jayce appeared and said, "Mom. Do you really want to see this?"

I jumped up out of the uncomfortable chair with alacrity. "Yay! Yes! Can I?" and he indicated that he'd been buffaloed into allowing this by my dear friend.

"I listen to her," he told me. "I don't always listen to you, but I listen to her."

It takes a freaking village, people.

Back we went to one of those cell-like little rooms in the rabbit warren that is Children's Hospital and a sweet nurse named Katie talked him through the process of giving himself his first injection in detail. He did brilliantly, administering the shot like a pro with only a little bit of guidance, and I got it on video with eight percent left on my phone battery, and we both teared up just a teeny bit when it was over. I was wicked proud and I am incredibly grateful to Michelle for her persistence.

The next week it came to pass that although he had in fact done a fabulous job with the first shot, he really had no clue what he was doing and was nowhere near ready to be independent with this process and needed some more coaching to get the whole thing right. And so, being me, I got creative.

I spent a little time with my sewing machine and a few scraps of leftover fabric and created a brand new accessory for the trans guy on the go: a Bag of Manhood. This is a little drawstring bag that holds a bottle of testosterone, some syringes and needles, and some alcohol wipes and cotton. In order to infuse the Bag of Manhood with the proper masculine energy, I swore a lot while making it. I also didn't measure anything or follow any instructions, because Real Men Don't Do That. I just stuck fabric to other fabric and sewed until it looked like a bag. Add drawstring and voila.

I also created a little instruction sheet he can use as a guiding document for preparing and administering his own shots. It starts with *Gather Your Crap!* and ends with *Congratulate Yourself*! He's getting pretty good at it by now, especially that last step. He only needs a little bit of cueing to get liquid instead of air into his syringes, and he does the actual shot part like a boss.

When you start T they hand you this packet of information about it that will either motivate you to dive the hell in or just scare the crap out of you. We now have seven dwarfs of testosterone therapy, too. These are: Hungry, Hairy, Horny, Ouchy, Stinky, Pissed, and Dysphoria.

A couple of months after he started T he was about three and a half dwarfs in. He had a friend at school who upon learning that he had just gotten started on T brought him five slices of pizza one night at work with, "Dude. You're gonna need these."

I thought he ate a lot of food before he started. How little I knew. He also stated that he was looking forward to more of Hairy Dwarf arriving because, "I might get eyebrows, Mom." I remain uncertain why he wanted big eyebrows, but I suspect the reason is jealousy of Mari, who has eyebrows they can wield as actual weapons. They lower those eyebrows of theirs and people in the room become convinced they're about to charge like a bull and gore them. They're not wrong, either.

About three days after his second shot he came to see me going, "Ow. Everything hurts and I'm dying."

"What do you mean, everything hurts?" I put down my crochet project, a blanket I had named Yarn Futility in Lavender, and peered at him over the top of my glasses.

"Everything. Hurts?" he said in a condescending 'Mom, are you inhabiting your body today?' kind of voice.

Further questioning on my part elicited the information that he felt like he might feel the day after an eight-hour dance class. Stiff, sore, and generally beat up. "Ow," he said again in case I'd missed it the first time.

One scary but relevant piece of information here is that some types of psychiatric medications can cause really severe muscle aches and that these side effects are sometimes a sign of dystonia. Dystonia is characterized by involuntary muscle contractions or spasms and can be progressive and even permanent, resulting in difficulty walking, breathing, and speaking as well as involuntary positioning of the limbs in abnormal postures. Atypical antipsychotics like the one he is on do show this in the list of *rare but serious* side effects, so I was watching him closely.

At this point I decided I needed to do some more digging into the research on testosterone side effects in trans guys. I know at this point in the book, dear readers, it will not come as much of a shock to you to discover that most of this research is largely nonexistent or at best woefully incomplete. So I turned to a fabulous Facebook group I am part of called *Serendipitydodah For Moms of Trans Kids*. The group consists of a bunch of moms who are trying to walk the Yellow Brick Road of raising our transgender babies without veering off into the poppies too many times. Boy, is there a lot to learn. These moms talk about absolutely every aspect of life with and for our trans kids, from gear to treat dysphoria, to clinic and doctor recommendations, to school related issues.

"My son complained about growing pains the whole first year he was on T," said some moms. "Oh yes, muscle aches are a thing they don't tell you much about," said others. I relaxed a little bit more when I found some information indicating that since testosterone literally remodels the body, a certain amount of discomfort is to be expected especially at the beginning of therapy.

Depending on what age they start T, trans guys get an increase in muscle mass and a redistribution of their body fat to produce a more masculine physique relatively early in treatment. One source I found said that even if a boy is an adult when he starts therapy he can get about an inch of growth just from the effect of new muscle on his spine.

This means that starting testosterone is literally like putting a guy on a medieval torture rack. Remember the executioner/torturer guy from Count Rugen's Pit of Despair in *The Princess Bride*? Albino dude, kind of scary looking, didn't say a whole lot but generally seemed satisfied with his work? If you haven't seen it, put the book down and go watch it. I'll wait. Anyway I keep picturing that guy showing up in Jayce's room every night when he's zonked out on Trazodone and setting him on the rack and going S-T-R-E-T-C-H. No wonder he walks around yelling, "Ow" all the time.

Aside from the muscle torture and other side effects, the drug does have some beneficial effects that we noted quite early on. Guys on T are supposed to get quite a bit stronger physically. One night just before his third shot he called excitedly up the stairs to me.

"Hey Mom!"

"What?"

"It's working! I can open my own soda!"

My friends all want me to rent him out to them to open pickle jars, but NOBODY can open those things.

Jayce: Transition Tales

For a while, I thought I was going to have to be 25 before I would even be able to think about going on testosterone or getting top surgery. My former parents said I was way too young to make that decision and insisted over and over again that I was going to change my mind. Actually, for a while I wasn't really sure if I wanted to get on T. I went back and forth for maybe 2 years about the pros and cons of going on hormones, and for the longest time it was always more pro than con but the biggest thing I was considering was my voice dropping. The one thing I loved about myself pre-transition was my voice. I was a singer, I still am, I have always loved singing and songwriting and the one thing I truly did like about myself was the massive vocal range I had. I had heard stories from trans guys on the internet and guys I had personally known, that some of them were singers and they weren't able to sing like they used to, and some stopped singing and didn't enjoy it nearly as much, but others I talked to said they finally heard their voices the way they had always wanted their voice to sound. So, I was listening to male covers of songs on YouTube one night, and that's when I decided, I am ready for my voice to sound like this. That's when I said "Mom! Dad! Anna! Peter! Whole damn world! I'm going on T!" and every single one of them said "'Kay!"

Eventually we got an appointment at Children's, and I was shocked to find that all I had to do was get some labs done and sign the consent forms. I had no idea it would be this easy. I was pleasantly surprised. The day I got on T was actually the same day a close friend of mine, a 14-year-old trans kid, died by suicide. I couldn't help thinking on that day that he should have been able to get to this amazing milestone too.

It's a fantastic milestone, but I was still reluctant to have my mom be in the room while this was happening. I didn't think it was a big deal, I didn't think she'd actually want to see it. For the longest time I didn't think I'd ever be supported if this ever even happened. It seemed that my mom was working behind the scenes, because I got a text from Anna Pesce's mom Michelle (and thank you Michelle). She told me in no uncertain terms that I needed to let my mom record my milestone moment, period. Somehow Pesces have power over me. If you're a Pesce and you tell me what to do, I am likely to listen. I don't always listen to my mother, but Michelle says as long as I listen to one of the mothers it's all good.

I got my mom and kind of sighed and reluctantly and sarcastically said "So you really wanna see this?" She just *jumped* out of her chair, going "Yeah!" and now I am really grateful she was there to share this with me, because I never thought I would have support for starting testosterone.

I did my own first T shot, with coaching from the nurse. I have never been one to care about shots, I'm fine with them, and I was very happy once it was done. The second I got that shot I just relaxed. I felt much more like me even though nothing physical had changed yet.

My voice didn't drop in a day, I didn't get a beard in a day, but quite quickly I was sore. It was good because one of the ways you know T is working is when you can no longer fit into any of your clothes, because the shape of your body is changing. This does cause a fair amount of muscle aching, though.

One of my first and best victories was when I hollered at my mom from downstairs "Mom!" And she was like "OMG what did you do now?" and I was like "I can open my own soda!"

So if you're on T and can suddenly open your own soda, you know the hormones are starting to work.

Chapter 18

Kelly: Hamper Diving 101

They say that clothes make the man. I don't know who 'they' is in this case, but whoever 'they' are, 'they' are full of crap right to their eyes. Jayce's idea of sartorial splendor involves matching socks. Or, really, any socks.

Remember the clothes shopping trip? The one where the cashier looked at us and asked if we wanted to keep the hangers and we just laughed? Jayce got a lot of clothes that day. He got enough stuff so that it meant he didn't have to do laundry for a long time. I mean like a really long time. He's only got the one set of sheets, so I have to get on his case somewhat regularly about those, but clothes he's got.

Once in a while I wander into his room and say something pointed about laundry and a few weeks later (moms of boys, you relate to this, I know you do) he reluctantly carries one small basket up the stairs, bitching about how he needs to rig up a drone of some sort to fly it all up there for him, because THAT would somehow take less time. Fortunately when he bitches about laundry or schoolwork or whatever it is, he does so in this relatively good-natured way that goes, "Crap. I don't want to do this, Mom! Why are you making me? Is it because you want me to succeed? So I can get educated and meet Emma Watson? Crap."

We got him a dresser for a really good price from Paula Langhorst, one of the friends that also kicked in to help buy his glasses. This thing could hold three or four corpses in a morgue. It's like the huge dresser from Pippi Longstocking's attic where she keeps all her treasures. When I was a kid I wanted nothing more than to be allowed to rummage through that dresser. This piece of furniture in Jayce's room is similar. It's absurdly heavy, for one thing. We had to get the neighbors to play Sherpa for us to get it up the steps and into his room. They did so willingly enough but I probably owe them all beer or something.

The top of the dresser is covered in Lego creations from Harry Potter. He's got the Hogwarts Express up there right now, a snake thing he says is the basilisk, and Hogwarts Castle. It's a highly useful, functional piece of furniture, and the irony about dresser drawers is that they are basically attractive laundry baskets that fit in a big wooden box thing.

"Jayce, you really need to run some laundry." I had wandered downstairs and peered in at him one recent morning when he was awake and actually sitting upright.

He looked around the room and at the baskets of clothes sitting on the floor. "Some of this is clean," he informed me. "Like, a basket and a half." A basket and a half. How is this a thing? If you mix dirty clothes with clean clothes the clean clothes are no longer clean. They instantly become dirty clothes by virtue of their proximity to the blech that exists in a pile of teenager laundry. Hell, they might instantly become dirty clothes just by being in the same room, even if they're not actually touching.

"How do you know which ones are clean and which are dirty?" I asked this because despite my obvious general wisdom, I am apparently not quite as smart as I think I am, because as these words were leaving my mouth I knew exactly what the answer would be—pick them up and sniff. (Boy moms, you're still with me here, do not bother denying it… please?)

Having four kids in the house creates the potential for a whole lot more chores that need done. Some chores seem to increase in volume, like laundry and dishes and taking out garbage. More people equals more laundry, dishes and garbage. Also there is this weird entropy that starts to set in once you begin allowing, say, junk mail to be put on a table. Set one catalog down figuring you'll look it over later and before you know it the table is collapsing under the weight of twenty three other catalogs, a phone book that somehow ended up brought into your house despite the existence of Google, a plastic bag that contains six sequins and an open bottle of Elmer's glue that has leaked all over the inside, the nutrition information panel from a frozen pizza you tore out for your carb counting journal, the aforementioned carb counting journal that is completely blank except for a large Hershey's Syrup stain on the front, two paper clips, and the six empty toilet paper rolls you are saving for a kid's school project.

As quickly as some things get filled, other things get emptied. The contents of things like cereal boxes and milk jugs seem to evaporate like dew. A child will leave exactly an eighth of a teaspoon of milk in the bottom of the jug and figure that since there's some left there's no reason why it needs to be removed from the refrigerator. This means that empty cracker boxes and containers of applesauce cups proliferate in the pantry and when the weekly grocery inventory time rolls around we think we still have food when, in reality, we have a whole bunch of empty boxes. The bathroom becomes completely devoid of shampoo, conditioner, and toilet paper almost as soon as it gets put in there. I think these kids believe there is a Toilet Paper Fairy who shows up in the middle of the night and puts new rolls of toilet paper on the shelf.

We actually do employ a cleaning service every other week. They do the real grunt work of mopping floors, cleaning bathrooms, and vacuuming the place. In order for them to vacuum they do need to be able to actually access the FLOOR, which means we all have to do at least a half-assed job of keeping it picked up. I love coming home after they've been here and finding everything smelling like lemon floor cleaner and all the trash emptied and sparkling bathrooms. Those are the best 4.8 minutes of my week. Very soon after they leave, though, that entropy creeps back in and people begin behaving like people around here.

Cue the Family Meeting And Chore Assignment night. Daniel finally cracked completely after watching a child walk away from the kitchen leaving a sink full of dirty dishes on a cleaning day. This led to a discussion with me about how the parents in this equation were dying of overwork and the kids were… not. So I called a Family Meeting.

Jayce is not used to the Family Meeting as a way of solving problems. To be honest we hadn't done it that often either because usually whatever issue was happening tended to be a one or two person dilemma, but we were faced with a six person Full Clan Disaster here and so they all trooped into the living room. I called the meeting to order by banging my gavel (a stuffed tiger Gabi got at American Furniture Warehouse) on the podium (okay, the cat carrier.) The upshot of all this was that every kid got a new job that he or she was responsible for and we got to supervise, harangue, harass, remind, inspect, exhort, and rant at them to see that they all did their assigned jobs. Eventually the meeting was adjourned with the tiger gavel, which made a surprisingly satisfying sound when rapped firmly on the cat carrier.

Okay, I pick on Jayce a lot in this book but here I really have to give the kid a plug, because he will dive in and do pretty much anything I ask him to do if two basic conditions are met: One, if he understands the *reason* he is being asked to do whatever it is, and two, if I can get him to laugh while asking. I am hilarious, so this generally works. He and I are currently teamed up for kitchen maintenance and food shopping and preparation. Since we did this, he voluntarily washes pans with soap and actual warm water and he goes grocery shopping with me cheerfully once a week even though I do make him leave the house while it's still morning. He'll take on the job of making lunch for the little kids without being asked, he routinely takes them up to play at the park, and he cleans the grease off the stove. No, really. He cleans. The grease. Off the stove. Single ladies, I will do my level best to get him to love laundry, but I'm telling you, he is the total package.

I admit it's also rather freeing to tell the kids that Kaiden's washing, drying, and sorting their laundry, but they're responsible for putting it away. Folded or not, I don't care. Mismatched socks, inside out, I have lost interest. If it's off the floor I'm completely satisfied, and if you can't find your particular favorite T-shirt, oh well. If the dishwasher's clean but needs emptied, that's Mari's job and you can safely ignore it. Cat box scooping is on Gabi. If a cat barfs in one of their rooms, that becomes their personal cat barf and they deal with it.

Dialogue with Jayce a minute ago: "I have nearly a hundred pages of this book!"

"Wow, that's a lot!" he said. "Cool!"

"Yeah," I told him, "but I've run out of material for the moment."

He thought for a second, shrugged, and said, "Well, I could complain some more."

The. Total. Package.

Jayce: If You Can Still Walk In My Room, It's Clean Enough

I've never been one that has actually liked to do chores. If you have ever met a teenage child who likes to do chores, please let me know who they are. At my old house I would have to be begged and begged to do the simplest things, like unload the dishwasher or put a glass in the sink or whatever. My former father would be really petty and he would punish me for leaving my socks on the floor by taking TV away for a week. Really disproportionate. Enough of that happened that I gave up on doing chores completely. They could take away whatever they wanted, I was just not going to do it anymore. Nothing they could do was gonna make a difference. I was past the point of no return.

In the Price household, though, I have no problem doing things and contributing to the family, because get this: I actually love and respect them. I think that was part of the problem with my former parents, I didn't love and respect them. I didn't have any motivation to do anything I was obligated to do. There was no satisfaction in that.

I'm expected to do things around here like clean my room, do the laundry, clean public spaces I use like the basement, things like that. I'm also glad to do extra things like take my siblings to the park or fix them lunch. I'm glad to do things here and there that are extra helpful. But getting me to do my own laundry is a task. I always say, "I'll get to it someday, why don't you start spring cleaning now and I'll catch up to you in the fall." Around my own room and my own laundry you have to hassle me a lot more than anything else around the house.

It got the point where I was doing generally what I was supposed to, and the little kids were doing things here and there, but it all of us could have been contributing more. So, Mom called a family meeting.

Family meetings at my former house were awful, there was always screaming and yelling, and our family therapist would literally put herself physically between myself and my former mother, acting as a barrier to try to minimize the screaming and make sure we didn't hit each other.

When we did it at the Prices it was a pleasant surprise. We even had a little fun with it, because Mom kicked things off with her tiger gavel and cat carrier. I didn't realize until now that meetings could be constructive and we could all get our voices heard and nobody had to get screamed at in the slightest.

The word "consequences" has a totally different meaning in the Price household too. When I was growing up, there would be screaming and hitting, or losing a privilege for a ridiculous amount of time for almost nothing. Not putting a dish in the sink meant I didn't get to practice driving when I was getting my permit. Apparently, I had to be perfect to get any kind of freedom.

Around here, the word "consequence" means you pick up an extra chore, which is way better than what I did before. I will screw around and give you crap about laundry, and I will bitch about stuff, but I bitch while I am doing the extra chore. As long as it gets done, I really don't think the Queen (Mom) cares.

Chapter 19

Kelly: The Bullshit Gets Deeper

One of the first bureaucratic errands Jayce and I ran together was a trip to his college's Office of Financial Aid. The purpose of the trip was to talk to them about getting him a thing called a Dependency Override. This is a document that allows financial aid to be awarded to a student based solely on the student's income and not on that of their parents. A dependency override is surprisingly hard to get, because as a student even if your parents decide they are spending all your college money on a new pool for their backyard or a trip to Bora Bora, you are considered their dependent for financial aid purposes until you hit the ripe old age of 24. In order to obtain a dependency override you have to be leaving your parents' home under what the system calls 'Extraordinary Circumstances'. We figured our situation qualified as unusual enough and so off we went.

We were sitting in the office there waiting for somebody to come and get us and this lady popped out and called out a name that was (and is) completely wrong and Jayce stood up. "Really?" I thought, "What the actual hell?" And this little sad feeling came over me that got exponentially worse when I looked at Jayce and saw his dispirited demeanor. He drew himself up taller and said, "I go by Jayce, it's in the paperwork." The lady apologized and said oops, she'd fix that, but the damage for the day was done. I knew too much and I needed the Men In Black to come get me and zap me with that little LED thing they use to erase people's memories.

If you get married and want to change your name, the process is almost pain free. You do need to make a visit to the Social Security office, but you can drive over there in your still-decorated car that now says *JU T MARR ED* and still has tin cans clanking merrily behind it, hand them your marriage certificate, and people will say, "Congratulations!" and mail you a new card in a week or so. You can go to the DMV and get your driver's license redone with no more than the usual DMV related hassles. You might have to listen to some sloths telling jokes like they did in *Zootopia*, but waah, no big deal.

Trying to change your name at any other time is moderately excruciating.

First of all, ALL THE WEBSITES WILL BE WRONG. Like, literally all of them. You will go out to your own county's website to find the right forms and fill them out in painstaking detail and follow all the instructions, and you will still be at the courthouse on the wrong day or at the wrong time or with the wrong ID or the wrong forms filled out the wrong way, and a nice clerk with glasses halfway down her nose will peer over them at you and say, "This is all different now." Then she will look at you and ask, "Did you get this information from our website? It isn't hard to find."

Try not to cry, it's pointless.

Eventually, if you're persistent enough and willing to spend enough time on hold, you will reach a human being who has a clue about what is going on. In Jayce's case this was a lovely human named Levitt at the TRUE Clinic, who is billed as a 'Navigator' and who connected us with the Colorado Name Change Project. These people are dedicated to helping transgender Coloradans navigate the crazy process that is required here.

Requirements vary by state, but here in Colorado you need to go get both a Colorado and a Federal background check and then submit those with the correct name change petition paperwork and a nice fat check and you're good. Sounds easy, right? Wrong!

The background checks are a major issue all by themselves. Jayce went to get fingerprinted at some fingerprinting place and they told him they'd send the cards and background check requests to both the state and Federal agencies. Cool. Awesome. He asked them how long it would take to get the results back and the agent said, "Wellllll… Colorado is pretty quick, but the FBI is running eight to ten weeks out." Seeing no other option, he paid the $69 and started the waiting process. Every day we'd check the mail for one of the two background checks, and every day, nada. Then finally, victory, the Coloradans stepped up and said, "Guess what? He's not a criminal!" Fifty percent of the job, done!

Wrong again.

The Colorado background check expires after ninety days. Apparently Colorado is worried that people who commit felonies have a quota to meet and must therefore average one felony every three months or lose their status as Gold Felony Club members. No felon wants this to happen, because the Gold Felony Club offers deep discounts on travel, car rentals, and restaurants nationwide, and once you drop out of the club it's hard to get back in. The waitlist is ridiculous, and if you get behind and have to commit two or more felonies in a single ninety day stretch it's very difficult to get one of them backdated. Colorado criminals are therefore extremely careful not to let their memberships lapse, hence the need for a frequent reevaluation of someone's professional miscreant status.

The Feds are less worried about this, and their background check expires after a year, probably because Federal crimes require more time, money and resources to commit. If you're planning a Federal crime you need to think carefully about things, like whether or not you'll be crossing state lines, who made the counterfeit currency engraving plates you're thinking of buying, and whether anyone will notice if Alfred E. Neuman is the face on your new forty-dollar bills, and so forth.

A few weeks into the wait for the FBI to get in touch, the idiot in the White House managed to trigger a government shutdown over a tantrum he had about a border wall, and suddenly FBI background checks became a thing that was 12 to 16 weeks out, and they were very sorry for the inconvenience.

They didn't sound sorry, but it was what it was, and so we did some more waiting.

Eighteen weeks went by and the Colorado background check had long since expired, and still we heard nothing from the Feds. We finally called the agency and stayed on hold for a really long time to get to an actual human being, only to be told that they'd never heard of Jayce and had no record of a background check request.

Ohhh-kay. Admittedly, it's kind of good when the Federal government's crime fighting machine doesn't go, "Oh, we've been looking for YOU, stay on the line so we can trace this call and don't try to run because roadblocks are already up." In certain circles it's wonderful news NOT to exist. In this case, however, it was just annoying as hell.

Apparently someone at the first fingerprint place had been focused not so much on their actual job as on their NCAA bracket picks (it was October, they wanted to get the jump on it) and whether to get Chinese or Thai for dinner. New rules in this state say that law enforcement people are no longer allowed to do your fingerprints for background checks in civil matters, which this ostensibly was, although by this point every time Jayce had to deadname himself to get a prescription filled he was feeling decidedly UNcivil. The person at the FBI was kind enough to refer Jayce to another fingerprint vendor and he made another appointment and off he went, got fingerprinted again and paid more money and the wait for the paperwork began a second time. By this time the FBI had instituted a plan that allowed Colorado peeps to get their prints done electronically, and ten days later we had both Colorado and FBI background checks in hand, and off we went to the courthouse, where they told us to come back on Tuesday at 1:00 because name changes were only done three days a week from 1:00 to 1:30. Oh, and by the way, all our forms were wrong.

Fourteen paragraphs chock full of bureaucracy have now gone by and Jayce still cannot legally be called Jayce. To make a long story even longer, eventually we got to the right courthouse on the right day at the right time with the right forms that were correctly completed, and Jayce was even wearing actual pants instead of his elderly basketball shorts. A miracle occurred and a judge decided he was rocking the pants and granted him not only his name change but his exemption from publication, and three minutes later Jayce Kennedy Price legally came into the world. A court clerk handed us three signed certified copies of the decree and we were out of there.

We celebrated this momentous occasion by going to Walgreens to change his name in the system so the pharmacy staff would quit calling him by his deadname when he refills his testosterone.

After you get your name change decree finalized, the next place the powers that be recommend you go is the Social Security office. They want to make damn sure they can track your ass down at tax time regardless of what name you've got, so you can contribute your share to America's high priority items like maintaining public open spaces and clean air and water and... no? Oh. Okay, so you can contribute your share to big oil and big pharma and military might. This paragraph is cynical and I debated revising it and then thought, nah.

This is a place that is simply bursting with bullshit. People generally do not go there to have a good time, although the world is full of weirdos and it takes all kinds. I have spent a lot of time thinking over the years (generally while sitting in government offices) about ways the government could raise a whole lot of money, and one idea I had was to offer spa treatments for a nominal fee at such places. You could go in, take your little paper number, realize you're gonna be there for the majority of the day based on the fact that they are serving A-6 and you have number Q-972, and have a pedicure or a facial or a chair massage. They could have canapés. I don't know about you, but that whole experience would be better if I could get a cup of fruit infused water and a delightful cucumber finger sandwich.

Anyway, Jayce and I headed off to the Great Taxpayer Identification Office to ensure that he was correctly identified. We got there half an hour before they opened so we'd be sure to be helped in the first six hours of the business day, took our number, and then went and sat down in the Cattle Pen. We were talking and being goofy as usual and Jayce looked over at me and then in a completely random moment of inanity one of the lenses of his glasses fell out and landed on the floor. There was no reason for this, it just happened. We looked a little closer at the glasses and realized that as usual Jayce had a screw loose – one of those tiny screws on the temple had disappeared. It is absolute bullshit that so much of our vision is dependent on the teensy little metal screws that hold our glasses together. There should be a better design, perhaps funded by the generous taxpayers of our great nation. These things are absolutely vital to our economy and our functioning as a country. Millions of people a day could be rendered blind by a supervillain with a strong enough magnet.

The Cattle Pen in the office consisted of a square segment of floor crammed with about 60 uncomfortable metal chairs that locked together and that were placed to provide roughly 2/3 the legroom provided on a zero-frills airline in coach. The only way to even SEE the floor involves contorting yourself into a weird sort of C-shape. We proceeded to bend ourselves around like pretzels for a minute or two and then the lady sitting next to me asked what we were looking for and Jayce said, "My glasses screw."

Everybody in there must have been incredibly bored or had no cell battery left, or both, that day, because within a couple of minutes we had a regular crowd of people helping us look for the damn screw. This became a united quest, like the search for the Holy Grail except much sillier. Given the amount of space available, the only way to accomplish the search was for several people to get up out of the way and several other people to situate themselves ass up between the rows. It looked like a demented Whac-A-Mole game in there, with different butts rising up out of the seats at different intervals in what seemed a completely futile effort to find a four-millimeter screw, which, when found at last, turned out to be stripped.

Nihilistic karma at its finest, folks.

Jayce: Just Call Me Jayce

Some people will try to tell you that the name change process is easy. If you get married that might be true, but if you're transgender and you're trying to match your name with your identity and get it all changed you would be wrong about how easy it is. I had a pretty good amount of patience for the name change process, because first of all, my parents were okay with it even happening. I was pretty agreeable throughout the process despite all the bureaucracy that was involved.

You have to get fingerprinted and you have to have proof that you are a really terrible criminal at both the federal and state levels. I believe we had to try this three times. The Feds said they had never heard of me, which is probably a good thing. It must mean you're not a really big criminal. It was amazing they even got fingerprints from me, because with my anxiety and ADHD I have practically chewed my fingertips clean off. I have no idea how they got anything from me at the fingerprint office.

We got the prints and were ready to start the court date process. We went to the courthouse and we had all the paperwork ready, and they were shocked that we did because most people don't. The day we went there they weren't hearing name change cases, so we went back maybe two days later to finally get everything processed. I was excited to get the court date to get this done, I had been waiting for a while. I decided my chances to get the name change granted would be better if I wore actual pants, and so I wore my gray jeans.

The judge was very nice and said sure, I think we can change your name, and we got the decree. It was the last time I had to say my deadname in front of official people, which to me seemed like something to celebrate.

After we got the actual piece of paper, we had to change my name all over the place in all kinds of systems. We had to change it at school, and at legal offices, and everywhere else I ever went. I could just hand them the paperwork and suddenly there was no deadnaming. I loved that.

As usual, my mom managed to corral a bunch of random strangers into helping her with the search for my glasses screw at the Social Security office. She just asks for stuff and people give it to her, I don't know how she does it. I texted my boss and told her about the situation. It was a very surreal thing to have to call in sick at work for, but she works with a bunch of college age guys so she's probably heard worse. I told her "Well, I was coming to work but I got caught up at the Social Security office with a screw loose, and now I can't see." Needless to say, this set of apparently unrelated statements required some clarification, but my boss knew me pretty well by that point and she was fine with just saying "Okay. Never mind. I don't need to understand."

Once again we concluded a Driving All Over Hell day with food. I got food, I didn't have to go to work, and it was a good day.

Chapter 20

Kelly: Trans Crap Tuesdays

Most people reading this book probably have a calendar someplace that tells them where they're supposed to be when and something about what they're supposed to do once they get there. I personally am completely dependent on Google Calendar to manage my life. Without it I am absolutely beyond screwed and with four kids to keep track of am guaranteed to end up missing major stuff. My phone has an alarm in it that goes off once a week to remind everyone in the world that it is Trans Crap Tuesday and therefore Jayce needs to do his weekly testosterone shot and also move in the direction of getting more bureaucracy managed. We liked the sound of Trans Crap Tuesday because 1.) it rolls off the tongue nicely, 2.) it means we have actual time built into our schedule to get necessary stuff managed, and 3.) it's funny. We take great pride and joy in doing things around here just because they are funny.

Trans Crap Tuesdays consist of Medical Trans Crap, also known as the weekly testosterone injection, and Bureaucratic Trans Crap, which consists of whatever governmental or educational bullshit is on the docket for the week. Sometime vaguely morning-ish, Jayce gets up and wanders into the kitchen to get the Injection Of Manhood completed for another week. He has this just about mastered at this point and can prep his shot without looking at the directions and with very little coaching from Nurse Mom over here. I can screw around on Facebook on my phone while he sets it up because I have reasonable confidence that he won't contaminate everything and have to start over. He did have a period of a few months when he just lost his nerve, but he's back to being able to do it for himself, usually by holding the needle poised and counting, "One, two, FUCK."

I have any number of mom friends who have been on godawful injectable medications like Lovenox or HCG because they were trying to get pregnant, stay pregnant, or both, and they tend to flap their hands at him impatiently and say things like, "Oh hell no, now let me tell you about how I had to take a shot in the ass every day for six months with a needle the size of a railroad spike and then drive to work over forty miles of bad road." Moms and sympathy aren't really much of a thing, because no matter what you've put up with, there's some mom out there who has had to contend with worse. Don't believe me? Find a way to listen in when a group of moms who have toddlers are standing around talking about their childbirth stories. Eventually you will hear things about fifty hours of back labor, C-sections that occur before the anesthetic kicks in, nine months of intractable vomiting, $50,000 worth of fertility treatments, and pooping on the table during delivery, all so the little fiend crawling around eating ants at the park can exist. We go through a lot for our kids, and we'll tell you about it in enough detail to make you go woozy and break out in a cold sweat. We're also completely without modesty by the time Kid 2 or Kid 3 arrives in the world, which means if you keep prattling on about your medical misfortunes for too long we might show you our stretch marks.

The day Jayce moved in here I broke out a little manila folder, stuck it on top of a filing cabinet, and started storing documents he might need in it. That day it had one document in it – The Contract. I can't remember at what age I had an entire notebook full of vital documents, but I know I was older than Jayce is now. After a couple of months of sticking bills, medical records, vital documents obtained under great duress, tax forms, and assorted other items in there, it became clear that I needed to organize it all much better and shove it all into a notebook, which has logically been christened the Jayce File. Gabi drew an especially goofy caricature of him for the front cover that I think captures him perfectly – wild hair, demented expression, really a lot of teeth. The notebook has several sections in it: Don't Lose This Crap, for things like birth certificate and Social Security card, Legal Crap, which holds affidavits and name change documents, Medical Crap with its associated subheading Trans Crap (self-explanatory), School Crap, Tax Crap, and Random Crap. Every time we get some new document that needs to be saved, we shove it into the Jayce File, and usually it gets filed in the appropriate

Crap Section. We are going to need to come up with an alternative to the notebook soon, because for one thing it is beginning to become hard to get the damn thing closed, and for another this one notebook contains everything a would-be criminal would need to not just steal his identity but to make it so completely Byzantine a task to put right that it would never get resolved.

The existence of this Big Book Of Jayce-Related Crap makes people smile who are normally not prone to doing so. People working at the DMV, usually so incorruptibly taciturn as to become self-parodies, have been known to make actual pleasant conversation with us as we wait for some form to come off the printer. "Who drew the picture on the cover of the book?" they ask, whereupon Jayce mutters something about how it really doesn't look like him at all and I tell them about Gabrielle's incisive talent for caricature. I have wondered whether or not TSA agents might respond in similar fashion, but have decided not to push my luck that much just to test a hypothesis that stupid. If Jayce gets that bored he can go do it.

Jayce: Shots

Coincidentally enough, I got to start T on a Tuesday. Bloodwork, surgery consultations, and a bunch of other crap also all got scheduled on Tuesdays, so now we call it Trans Crap Tuesday.

Usually I am not afraid of shots, but it's a completely different thing when you have to do it yourself. I ended up doing all kinds of incentive things, like I would get cat treats or marshmallows (I love both) if I did the shot, or I would hold a bottle of hot sauce on the injection site so I can pretend I'm numbing the area. Things like that make T shots easier. I did have three or four months I couldn't do it myself and I would have to say, "Mommy stab me," which is a thing every mother wants to hear. Then I eventually got it back and now I do them all myself again.

While we were in the process of getting me on T, everything was happening at once, I had all these transition goals. We were working on the T and the name change and finding a surgeon all at the same time.

One of the things I needed to secure my job while I was with the Prices was my social security card. There might have been another way to get hold of it, but the most efficient way seemed to be to try to get the original. I had contacted my former parents and I'd told them that I needed the card because I needed to get this job. They suggested I come meet them at their house, and there was no way in hell that was happening. I also needed backup, so I said to them meet me at the HR office at school, and bring the card.

They finally agreed to that plan, reluctantly, and so I said "Price!" which was what I used to call my mom, "Get in the car, we gotta go get my social security card!" She was on it.

When we got there Kelly was on stakeout in the car and I had to go in and see what I could get accomplished.

I saw my former father. He was walking down the hall, and he'd made it his damn mission to make sure I gave him back the card so he'd be able to tell his wife that he was successful and they were going to remain in control of me yet again. It really pissed him off when that didn't happen. It satisfied me quite a lot.

We went to the HR office and my dad was holding onto the card as long as he possibly could. I took it and gave it to the lady to process my paperwork, and when that was done he said, "Give it back to me, you're not leaving this office until I get the card back." And then he shoved me. I said "Do that again, I have no problem telling the lady behind the desk to call campus security. No security officer is going to tell me at age 18 that I have to give you back the card, I'm an adult and it's legally mine."

He knew this and he wasn't happy about it. That was the first time I ever really stood up to him.

I said, "This is what's gonna happen. I'm keeping the card, it's mine. You should know better than to pick a fight with me on a college campus." He reluctantly stepped aside. I didn't even know where I was in the building, I just took the nearest back door exit and I figured I'd find my way back to the parking lot and it didn't matter if I had to walk a whole mile because I'd gotten it! And I still couldn't believe I had actually done something for myself that was that big.

I got back to the car where Kelly was and she was so panicked because she didn't know where I was or what was happening. She didn't have any text updates from me. I said, "By the way, I got it."

We were very victorious in the car, we kept yelling "FUCK yeah!" because it was something to celebrate that I had done that. Truly a badass day.

Chapter 21
Kelly: Birthday Parties, Naming Ceremonies And Momma McCracken

If you're a trans kid, your name is very, very important to you. Seeing his correct legal name on official identification documents like birth certificate, driver's license, and so forth is a big deal for Jayce. Every time he gets out an ID card he gets a little thrill now because he doesn't have to cover up his deadname to prevent people from seeing it. It's a beautiful thing.

One place where someone's name should really be correct is on the annual pastry offering that is a quintessential natal anniversary tradition in this country – the birthday cake. There are whole shows on television dedicated entirely to seeing who is most willing to absolutely kill themselves making a perfect birthday cake for some wealthy person. These things invariably have towering sugar sculptures with delicate lacy detail or life size fondant Great White sharks or working roller coasters made of Rice Krispies treats and glued together with the blood, sweat, and tears of the bakers.

I am not, as I have mentioned, a fabulous cook. I can sort of bake if the consumer is not terribly pretentious or demanding, and luckily my kids tend to descend upon anything I bake with high enthusiasm. Imagine, if you will, the reaction of a pack of wolves if somebody got a pastry bag and wrote "Happy Birthday Fang!" on a dead moose and plunked it down on the forest floor and you've about got it. They go "Cookies!" and there's this sort of terrifying blur of activity in the kitchen, and then I'm awash in a sea of crumbs and one small chocolate chip that rolls gently off the counter, spins for a moment on the floor, and is devoured by the dog.

If you've never seen Cake Wrecks it is a wonderful time-waster of a website on which people post examples of really awful cake decorating faux pas for all the world to see. You get to see pictures of cakes that say things like "Happy Birthday Bitch" because somebody can't quite make the name "Beth" correctly with a piping bag. They have whole sections devoted to whatever holidays you want to look at, from "Happy Morial Day, We Rember" to "Happy Falker Satherhood!" You can have a wonderful time giggling at the complete ineptitude of some people when they get hold of a bucket of fondant and some royal icing. My personal favorite has always been one that has a battalion of tiny plastic naked babies with Mohawk hairstyles riding carrots. What the hell the occasion was for that one I do not know, but for the better part of the last decade my life has been just a little bit better because I am aware of the existence of the naked Mohawk baby carrot cake.

What with one thing and another, it was very clear that this year's birthday cake for Jayce needed to be made by someone who was not me.

Enter my good friend Elizabeth Manzanares, who has a cake gig that she runs out of her kitchen. It's a beautiful thing to be able to call up a friend and say, "Okay I need a really weird cake here…" and have her immediately be able to think of a way to not only make the thing every bit as weird as I could wish for but also make it a GOOD kind of weird, unlike any of the Easter Bunny cakes on Cake Wrecks. Plus it will be delicious.

Around the same time as Liz agreed to make the first birthday cake ever for my son that had the name "Jayce" on it instead of his deadname, my other good friend TC McCracken was hard at work on returning to her career as a stand-up comedienne. TC does this show in Denver at the Voodoo Comedy Playhouse in which she plays a character she calls "Momma McCracken." Momma's show takes place entirely in her closet, and it is bawdy, hilarious, extremely irreverent, and a hell of a lot of fun. Before her life as a comedienne, TC was a teacher in the program at Hackberry Hill that Kaiden was part of, which meant she had Kaiden for both kindergarten and second grade. For some reason after this she still continues to talk to me, despite the fact that I was kind of That Parent at the school. I am both profoundly grateful and vastly entertained by her continuing friendship. She is as funny as hell.

She was that one cool teacher who always showed up dressed up for whatever lesson she was teaching that day. She'd come to school in fishing garb, dressed like a literary or Dr. Seuss character, and bring props and tools to help her illustrate whatever concepts she was trying to drill into the heads of her charges.

TC knew that Jayce's birthday was coming up and she also knew something of his story, and she made the insane mistake of telling me she'd perform for free at the party.

I jumped on THAT plan like a starving flea onto a dog and the idea for Jayce's 19th birthday party was born. We rented out the Voodoo, made a guest list, got Liz going on the cake process, and issued invitations to friends and family. I played my cards close to the proverbial vest and kept Jayce completely in the dark, which resulted in his becoming convinced that I was planning to humiliate him completely and publicly. No amount of reassurance would prevail over this conviction he held. His friends who were aware of the plan were also totally intransigent when he asked them for details, a thing I appreciated a lot.

The day for the party arrived and we picked up the cake and schlepped everyone to the Voodoo, where TC worked her comedy magic by breaking out her Momma McCracken persona and talking about how traumatic it was for her fictional family when her daughter came out as a vegetarian. Afterward we ate a truly yummy cake with raspberry and vanilla crap in it and a good time was had by all. Brian Kennedy, for some reason, ended up stuck holding a giant stuffed frog for the entire show because TC came into the audience and handed it to him and he had no choice but to just roll with it.

Jayce's cake was absolutely immense, and it read "Happy Birthday Jayce" in one corner and "Holy Crap, You're 19!" in the other. The center decoration was music from Bea Miller's song *Fire n Gold*. It was beautiful.

A few weeks later, after we had accomplished the Herculean task of changing Jayce's name and gender marker on his driver's license, birth certificate, and Social Security card, we held a barbecue in the backyard and did a naming ceremony. We have always celebrated all kinds of other stuff, including "gotcha" days for Gabi and Mari to commemorate the days we finalized their adoptions, and Kaiden Independence Day to celebrate the day he got discharged from the neonatal intensive care unit. Jayce invited a bunch of friends over and we ate yummy stuff, and he also got to create a small conflagration on the patio and burn up his old name. He had created a certificate on the computer, and it was one of the worst things I had ever seen for sheer girliness. It was bright pink, with a ballerina on one side and a unicorn on the other, and little flowers all over it. I don't hate the color pink but there has to be a balance, it's more of an accessory color, and this thing was so pink it GLOWED. In the center it said "Jayce's Deadname" and "Most Godawful Girl EVER." It made a dandy little blaze. Probably toxic from all the pink ink, but once it caught there was a nice little fire there.

Once that had been accomplished, we gave him another certificate with his new name, Jayce Kennedy Price, and "Hey World, Hold My (root) Beer." This one had a jar of pickles labeled "Opened by Jayce, the Man," a cartoon guy bungee jumping, and the Scoville Heat Unit scale next to a photo of

Emma Watson, who as you know from a previous chapter is at the top of the chart.

We had some beautiful cupcakes that I decorated all by myself, too. They were pickle green, and they had letters on them that said, "Price Cult Meeting." Cake Wrecks would be proud.

Jayce: Birthdays

My 19th birthday was really important, because my family was trying to make up for a lot of years of bad birthdays. My eighteenth birthday was truly crappy, because I had come out as trans. My former parents said, "We're not getting you presents, we're not having a party, we're not doing anything for you because you decided to be a boy." My former mom had only ever wanted a girl. She'd made that clear to everyone from the day she got me, and I just wasn't a girl no matter how hard I tried. It hurt a lot, and I thought they weren't serious, because they had fed me empty threats my whole life and I thought they were just talking. I was wrong, they really did essentially ignore my birthday. They did get me a cake, but it had to have the wrong name on it or else no name at all.

My 19th birthday had to be really memorable because of this, and fortunately Mom knows people who can do just about anything. I got my own private comedy show that my mom's friend TC did for us. TC had written a show especially for my birthday just for my own friends and family. Peter's dad Brian was there and Anna next to me. We invited a few other people but those were the people I really wanted there. Anna was so busy, going back and forth between rehearsals and had so much to do but she made it work.

The birthday cake was the first cake I ever had that had my name on it. Like my actual name, no bullshit. It said, "Holy crap, Jayce, you're 19!" It was a music cake, it had the actual music to *Fire n Gold* by Bea Miller, one of my favorite songs by her. So much work went into that night. It was so awesome.

The celebration didn't end there, either. When I got my name changed we had to make it into a party. We invited a bunch of my close friends over and we had a family barbecue. I got to see some of my friends from high school and a lot of people that loved me and were really waiting for this to happen. We ate Dude Food and played ping pong and Anna and I got really competitive. It was such a fun time. I got to celebrate being myself.

We had to make it funny though. That certificate I created was absolutely the worst and best thing I ever made with my deadname on it. It was the first thing I had with my deadname on it that I actually liked! I would have liked it a lot less if I had kept it instead of destroying it, which was ironic.

I couldn't get the lighter to work to save my life. It was one of those childproof ones and apparently at that time, chronology notwithstanding, I was still a child. Everybody was waiting and I clicked and clicked and no flame appeared. Mom eventually helped me get it going. Having a dozen people standing around on a patio applauding a burning piece of paper was hilarious.

It was a really fun way to commemorate my name change and start my new life in this family as Jayce Kennedy Price, which is a name that I am SO proud of, and I am very fortunate now to really love my name and my birthdays.

Chapter 22
Kelly: Rube Goldberg as the Patron Saint of Parenthood

Murphy's Law says that anything that CAN go wrong, WILL go wrong. The universe can be a maddeningly perverse place, apparently filled with foibles and quirks that are designed solely to thwart the goals of mankind. Some Rube Goldberg devices are a lot of fun, where one event leads to other events until the whole thing either ends or comes full circle. If you haven't seen it go find the video of OK Go singing *This Too Shall Pass* from their album *Of The Blue Colour Of The Sky*. It was made in conjunction with a whole lot of people from Syyn Labs in Los Angeles, and it took thirty people more than an hour to reset the whole thing between takes. They made something very cool.

Other instances of Goldbergian drama are like what happened over here one night. Neither Jayce nor I can remember what the hell started the entire thing, but the upshot was that it was another night of Jaycequake action, complete with thoughts of self-destruction, thousand-yard death stares, and a trip to the crisis center (in which the counselor's name was not Jayce's deadname). We spent the entire evening fighting off the demons, finally got help from the pros, got home after 1:00 am, and headed to bed. I shut off all the lights, staggered upstairs, and collapsed, completely exhausted.

Five minutes later Jayce appeared in my room again. This nocturnal visitation was closely related to an experience all parents have at one time or another. Imagine that you are tiptoeing away after finally getting the little monsters who dare call themselves your heirs to sleep. All is calm and peaceful, and then you do something like connect with a door with your face in the darkness or step on a Lego or something similarly inane, and then you say "OW!" and the screaming begins anew and part of you dies.

"Jayce," I said blearily, trying to remind myself of the identity of the child. "What."

"You are not going to believe this, but I broke the bed."

After ascertaining that he could neither fix the thing independently nor sleep in it as it was ("It's all slanty...") I sighed resignedly.

"Okay, I'll be down in a minute."

On the way downstairs, groping along the railing in the darkness, I slipped in a pile of dog crap considerately left at the base of the stairs by my faithful hellhound Callie. How Jayce missed it, either on the way up or on the way back down, I have no clue, but miss it he did and the trap sprung on me instead. I didn't fall on my ass, but I did skate for a second or two and leave a slimy brown trail of stench that went a couple of yards across the hardwood.

Perhaps predictably, my immediate response was to be seized with the giggles.

"Jayce!" I was trying to whisper-giggle, and it really wasn't working, but I at least wasn't laughing hysterically and awakening the entire household. "Jayce! Come HERE, dude. HELP."

Crickets. Nothing. The boy had shut his bedroom door, leaving me with two choices, either holler or hop. I opted to hop, and swearing under my breath (sort of) I made my way the five feet to the stair railing in a series of ungainly little bounces. I stripped off my sock, then decided to hell with everyone and turned on the stairwell light so I could see further pitfalls in my path.

That mess attended to, I of course had to share the sordid tale of the dog crap in the night with Jayce, who also found it hilarious.

Laughter is the best medicine, so back up to bed I went, and maybe half an hour later I received yet another nocturnal visitation. In January of 2019, just prior to what would have been his 102nd birthday, Jayce's grandfather passed away. A few minutes after I fell gratefully into bed after the (unrelated) trip to the crisis center, Jayce came in again, sobbing and shaking because he had just gotten the news - over *social media*. Talk about the worst possible way to find out somebody you love died! After that I decided to just inflate the air mattress and crash in Jayce's room for the night, because sleep wasn't happening for either of us.

That night Rube Goldberg really had it in for us, but that's not always true. One conversation, meal, or small event can set a chain of other occurrences into motion that turns into Niagara Falls. We are frequently amazed by the small things we've done that have had gargantuan consequences. I'm gonna nerd you all up now and talk about weather butterflies.

Edward Lorenz was a twentieth century mathematician and meteorologist who did a bunch of work that showed conclusively that small changes in a system can lead to very big, dynamic consequences. He called this idea the Butterfly Effect and the basic upshot was that—metaphorically speaking—the development of a tornado could be influenced by something as small as the flapping of a butterfly's wings weeks earlier. Lorenz is the father of chaos theory, and I have got enough chaos going on that if he hadn't died in 2008 he'd have had a field day over here.

What if I hadn't texted Brian back when he messaged me about Jayce? What if Jayce had said "Meh, no thanks, I'm gluten-free and vegan" when offered the opportunity to eat noodles with a crazy lady he didn't even know? What if he'd never gone to Brian for help, or Daniel had said "Wow, poor kid, I hope he gets some help" instead of "So, where's he gonna sleep?" These are tiny things, and on a different day in a different place with different weather, events might have arranged themselves in a completely different way.

Jayce: Kelly Price as the Patron Saint of Parenthood

Over here we've had a lot of really crazy nights where it's just one thing after another, and there's a panic attack during the middle of the day and then there's a conversation I don't want to have, and there's just a bunch of stupid BS that keeps going and going and going. There was one night, I don't even recall what started it, but it was one thing after another, so I went upstairs and got Kelly in the middle of the night again. We talked through whatever was bothering me and I got ready to go to sleep at last, and that's when the bed disintegrated.

I have a cheap wooden bed frame my mom found on Craigslist, and the slats on the bottom have never been nailed to the frame. I have given up on trying to keep the bed together. Every once in a while it would just fall. I'm much better at destroying things than I am at fixing them, especially in the middle of the night.

My mom came downstairs, and she slipped in a mess left by my dog, and then I couldn't even remember what I was upset about because I was too busy making fun of her.

We have had a lot of those nights where we would start a conversation and all we needed to do was use our talent for stupid humor and get us laughing about whatever it was. For a while I just rant, and I don't even know what I'm ranting about, but if I talk long enough and we laugh long enough, the temporary demons go away and I can go to sleep. Note that Mom says she can actually sleep while I rant. She appears to be listening and will even make "Oh yeah?" and "Uh huh" noises in the right places while having no memory of anything I am saying. She says I do the same thing to her though, so turnabout is fair play.

It was a hellish night, and I had actually gone to the police station to file a report about an incident involving my former parents. I am not going into detail about that, but I couldn't even believe I was in a police station. I was like a caged lion, and so was my dad, and I was just really shaken up, and so I called Anna. I was like okay, I'm freaking out, I don't know what to do, and I love you and you have a talent for making me feel better so call me.

We got home and I ended up talking to her for like an hour, and she made me feel better, and I was calmer but still needed some support.

My mom and I started playing this dumb game after I got off the phone where you write down any question no matter how silly and the other person has to answer it, equally silly. One of my questions was "If we were stranded in Timbuktu for three months, what would we do?" My mom answered that one with "The first two months would be you trying to climb a tree somewhere to get a cell signal so you could text Anna. The last month would be you trying to build a cell tower out of coconuts." She was absolutely correct about this. We went back and forth for a while, and I finally got myself calmed down.

Mom went to bed and I was relaxing, scrolling through my phone at maybe about 1 am, and I came across this post on Instagram from my cousin saying my grandfather had died. He was a week from being 102 years old, and he'd passed away the week before. It was hysterics all over again, I was devastated and nobody had even bothered to tell me he had passed. I had to learn about it on social media from a cousin I barely knew! I couldn't believe the night I was having, so I went to Mom.

She said "Okay, so what's up?" and I was just sobbing, telling her my grandpa had died, and I couldn't believe nobody had even called to tell me. My former parents had contact info to tell me what was happening and they opted not to. All it did was hurt me. And all of this happened in one night.

Mom blew up the air mattress and came down to sleep in my room so I wouldn't be alone. All four of us know we can go get her anytime in the night and she will help. No wonder she complains that she doesn't get any sleep.

Chapter 23
Kelly: Using Bullshit To Cope With... Other Bullshit

This little treatise has now traveled a fair distance beyond the chapter on Tupperware and tears, and it might be easy by this point to think that we have all skipped blissfully off into the sunset, having rescued the dragon, slaughtered the princess, and gotten home before the last stroke of midnight. After all, a whole kaboodle of anecdotes have arisen since then, most of which are filled with lightly whimsical silliness.

Nope.

You can't process a grief like what Jayce has had to deal with in one session with your Reiki practitioner. The wounds left behind by the kind of trauma he has experienced are the kind that cause medical examiners on television to say "Wow, look at the size of that exit wound!"

Best practices are all well and good, but at bedtime after a long day, my natural goofiness tends to combine with my lack of filters and cause me to come up with crap that makes no sense whatsoever but somehow seems to sort of work. The gestalt of my personal worldview is heavily influenced by the entire canon of Mad Magazine satire and similar weighty and serious literary works. Added to this is a tendency to note absurd events in modern life and store them up for future use, and you end up with Price's Batshit Crazy Coping Catalog.

Not long ago, Jayce was trying to deal with some really big shit. His usual path to dealing with such things generally starts with trying to totally ignore them. He will decide he is simply not feeling these things, or if he is feeling them that they are not that bad, or that if they are that bad he can stop feeling them anytime he wants.

He is invariably proven wrong, and then we all try to help him get through it with love, willingness to walk with him so he doesn't have to walk alone, and a liberal dose of what in this case will be literal bullshit.

One recent night he was lying flat in bed holding his phone directly above his face and sending texts to Anna's mom Michelle about how to handle his emotions. Kaiden and I were both in the room with him at the time, but like teenagers everywhere he was ignoring the people actually present in favor of texting the people who were somewhere else. The position he was in looked extremely awkward, as though he were an astronaut awaiting liftoff on the pad at Cape Canaveral and checking his Instagram feed before the wi-fi signal tanked.

"Hey Kaiden," I asked. "How do you think he does that? I'd drop the phone on my face."

"I know!" he said. "Me too!"

"Maybe we should make a betting pool. We'll get people to guess when he'll drop the phone on his face, and then whoever comes closest will get the prize money."

Jayce acknowledged this with an eyeroll that could be heard several counties away.

"You people would just smack the phone out of my hand and take the prize," he said dejectedly.

Well, this was of course patently untrue, because for one thing, trying to smack a phone out of a teenager's hands when that teenager is intent on hanging onto it requires more force than I can generate. I would need a machine of some sort.

"No," I told him, "it would have to happen naturally, like Chicken Shit Bingo."

He quit texting and peered out at me from under the phone. "What the hell, Mom, is Chicken Shit Bingo?"

Realizing I also had Kaiden's undivided attention, I then proceeded to describe this traditional and venerable game.

"You divide a floor up into squares like a bingo game and sell each square for money, and then you let a chicken wander around on the squares, and if it craps in a square whoever owns the square wins."

217

They looked at me like I had just described the single most idiotic thing they had ever heard, which is pretty much exactly correct. Granted, teenagers sort of look at parents that way all the time, but in this case the intensity of the "God, Mom, that is so dumb" stare was near the top of the scale. I decided to expand on my topic, because teachable moments come rarely and when you get one you have to jump on it.

"In California, when I lived there, they played the same game, except with cows. It needed a bigger field, and it took longer, but yup, cows."

Naturally at this point all sorts of questions cropped up about the finer nuances of the game. What happened, they wanted to know, if the cow shit landed on a line? Did the Bingo field have boundaries, or could the cow wander just a teeny bit outside the lines and crap in open, unowned territory, thus causing the game to slow down while somebody went and got a fuller cow? Were you allowed to scare the cow in an attempt to expedite things? How much of an effect did bovine diet have on the game? Would it be possible to feed the cow enough laxative material so that when the shit hit the floor it would simply explode and cover four squares? How far should spectators stand from the field to avoid the splash zone? Would there be a premium charged for upwind seating at the event? Was the honor system, in the form of a farmer in waders walking out into the field and hollering back "SQUARE B-5!!" acceptable, or should the game be judged via drone camera to ensure accuracy? Would there be a place for instant replay, and if so, what the hell for?

Jayce then wanted to know whether it would be possible to play with a cow and a chicken at the same time. This of course led to the question of what would happen if the cow shit ON the chicken? Double prizes? Maybe a bonus prize for whatever poor slob had to wash the chicken? And what if the opposite condition occurred? Imagine the chicken, showing incredible ingenuity and technological aptitude, carrying a ladder onto the field in its beak, propping the ladder against the cow, clambering up, and *pooping on the cow!*

Well, in the course of this analysis, Jayce became completely distracted from his emotional upheaval for a little while, and while I don't know for certain whether he went to bed that night contemplating barnyard animals enriching the soil with their evacuations, I like to think he did. For myself, the entire interlude produced a very odd dream in which Jayce was participating in a new sport called Synchronized Goat Jangling, in which goats wearing bells that played specific musical tones were trained to jump over things in a certain sequence and timing, causing the bells to play a tune. Jayce for some reason was an expert in Beatles songs. If anyone invents this sport in real life, get in touch, I will pay the upwind seat premium.

Jayce: More Bullshit From Mom

You may have guessed by now that we handle a lot of things with humor. There were many, many nights, more than I can count, where my emotions were unstable, I was just trying to figure out how to handle it, so one evening I was texting Anna's mom Michelle and maybe Anna as well.

I was focused on what those people had to say rather than what my mom and Kaiden had to say, because God knows I've heard enough from them.

Then my mom started talking in this random way about a game that is a real thing called Chicken Shit Bingo. That was one of the dumbest things I had ever heard in my entire life. It had never occurred to me that people would entertain themselves in such completely asinine ways. Of course, it was absolutely clear that if there were such a game being played, my mom would know about it, because that's just how she is. All of these things got me distracted, which was the point, from whatever was going on. I forgot what I even was texting Michelle about, I was laughing so hard.

This is one of the things my mom and my brother do best, they distract me from whatever is causing pain and I laugh and feel a lot better. A silly joke can go a long way.

After that, my mom had a dream that I had a talent for something called synchronized goat jangling. This was the product of her warped, twisted brain, and I wouldn't put it past her to one day invent it in real life. I was apparently skilled at Beatles songs. I have no idea why, I don't even like the Beatles.

I also had a dream that led to another inside joke. I had a dream where I was leading a dance choreography section at my dance studio, and you were supposed to dance and pick a partner. In my dream, when the music stopped you had to stop dancing and go outside and find a bug. It had to be a live bug. I told my mom about this and then my mom, like always, started coming up with ways she could cheat. She wanted to know if she could scuffle her hands across the floor and pick up some lint, pretend she had a bug and win, or if she could smuggle a dead bug in and pretend it was alive by doing some weird bug puppetry thing. The more bugs you catch the more points you get. Anna and I were fantastic at bug choreography, and the whole thing led to the creation of a really silly series of dance moves that my mom and I just simultaneously break into. People look at us like we are crazy. It's a good thing nobody ever said our choreography had to be good.

Chapter 24
Kelly: Dr. Google And Other Folks Who Should Never Give Medical Advice

If you've ever been diagnosed with any kind of chronic medical condition, you know exactly what happens as soon as you divulge that information to the world. An instantaneous outpouring of highly questionable medical advice will swamp your inbox. You will drown like a rat in a rain barrel.

"Go gluten-free," one well-meaning friend will say. "It absolutely changed my life. In fact, my eyelashes are so much better now than ever before. Wheat is poison."

"Have you been vaccinated?" another will inquire. "I know they SAY vaccines are safe, but I have a friend who has another friend whose cousin's sister's kid came out as transgender right after they got that Gardasil thing and I just don't think it's a coincidence."

Here in Colorado, medical marijuana has been a thing since 2000 and recreational use has been legal since 2014. It is a two billion dollar a year industry here, and weed tourism has become a big deal along with all the other cool things to do and see here. You can come to the Mile High City and literally get high. As a result of this, cannabis products have been seen as a cure-all for every condition from eczema to cancer, and if you mention that you have back pain, trouble sleeping, anxiety, or almost anything else, six people will immediately message you to say that you really do need to try this new strain of Alaskan Thunderfuck sativa because it will absolutely revitalize you. You'll be nineteen again, careening through life in that careless oblivion of your own fallibility that is the main luxury of youth.

If you had a time machine and could get to St. Paul, Minnesota before 2002, you could have visited a cool place called the Museum Of Questionable Medical Devices. This guy named Bob McCoy had collected a whole bunch of things that cause people now to shake their heads incredulously at the idea that a foot powered breast enlarger or a vibratory chair could cure whatever ailments you might have. Some of the items Bob collected came from the Battle Creek Sanitarium in Battle Creek, Michigan. The San, as it was sometimes called, was run by the Kellogg brothers, John Harvey Kellogg and Will Keith Kellogg. Their legacy today includes Kellogg's Corn Flakes, which were part of the diet program. Other options there included hydrotherapy, thermotherapy, electrotherapy, and a shitload of enemas (see what I did there?). The existence of this place is a testament to the crazy stuff people will do to themselves in the name of good health.

Being transgender is not a "lifestyle choice" as some people believe, it is a chronic, lifelong condition that without treatment can be incredibly debilitating or even fatal. There is a whole lot of real research showing that people who are transgender tend to have brain structures that actually match the gender they identify as, regardless of upbringing or genitalia. If you're trans, you need medical people on your side who are truly interested in promoting and preserving your health. You also need to listen to your friends with a critical ear. Which brings me to a story.

A while back Jayce was having a conversation with an old friend that he recounted to me later on. He made the mistake of telling me this story when we were in the swimming pool and I laughed so hard I nearly drowned.

"Mom," he said. "should I ask the surgeon who is doing my top surgery to try to preserve nipple sensation?"

"Why wouldn't you?" I asked him.

"Well, my friend told me that I should do it because if I don't have nipple sensation I won't know what temperature it is."

I stopped cold. "Um. What temperature it is? Like outside? Or what?"

He swore that his friend was absolutely serious and that he'd said that without nipple sensation, the ability to discern temperature would be a thing that Jayce would lose for sure and this would negatively affect his quality of life forever.

My brain being what it is, I instantly started picturing people everywhere using their nipples as thermometers in every possible situation. Need to know if your soup is cool enough to eat? Whip out a boob and dip it in. Want to check the temperature of your shower before committing yourself? Stick a nipple in there and you'll be good to go.

"Hey Jayce," I asked. "Maybe at your next surgery appointment you can ask the surgeon if she can set you up so one nipple is a thermometer and the other is a barometer, and then we can stick a propeller beanie on your head and use you for a weather station." Ever since then every time somebody wants to know what is happening outside we all yell "JAYCE! COME TELL ME THE TEMPERATURE!" He might be getting tired of this, but the rest of us are still enjoying ourselves, which is all I need.

Jayce: Okay, so I'm a weather station

One of the next major steps to getting my transition completed was getting top surgery. For maybe a year we were consulting with a few surgeons to try to get this process going. I had found one at Children's that I liked and we were ready to move forward. We thought we would choose her to do the procedure.

Part of the process is that you answer a million questions and they throw a bunch of information at you, most of which I fortunately already knew. There are a lot of options and a lot of things to consider.

For those of you who don't know, there are different procedures for top surgery. There is a procedure called keyhole where they cut the nipple off and remove the breast tissue through the hole they create. There's periareolar surgery, or "peri," which is where they do the same thing with a wider incision where they remove the tissue from around the areola. These are options for people with smaller chest sizes, and the doctor determines which procedure you will have based on your skin, your chest size, and how the doc thinks you will heal afterward.

I had what was probably the most common procedure type done, it is called double incision. With the other ones you don't have huge visible scars across your chest because the tissue is removed from the center of the breast, but with DI they make a large cookie cutter type incision around the breast, completely remove the breast tissue, and sew it back together. You're usually left with two very visible scars under the pec line.

Another thing they had us consider was whether or not we should at least try to preserve nipple sensation, which is easier for some people than for others. I was considering letting that option go, because they said it would be a cleaner procedure and I might get better cosmetic results if I didn't try to preserve nipple sensation, but I would also lose that erogenous zone completely.

I was thinking about this in the pool with my mom, and I told her that a friend of mine had said we should try to preserve nipple sensation because without it how can you tell the temperature? He was serious. I have known this guy my entire life and he was absolutely serious. My mom swears he was just messing with me, but I am telling you that was not the case.

We almost drowned laughing about it in the pool, and then as usual things got very silly. The stuff we kept coming up with just got weirder and funnier, and as usual we had people looking at us like we'd lost our minds.

I still haven't gotten my propeller beanie, though.

Chapter 25

Kelly: Love Poetry About Ostriches

"I'm gonna die alone," my kid said sadly one morning. This statement was somewhat incongruous given the three siblings, one mother, and one cat that had all invaded his room before he had even gotten out of bed. Of all the problems the boy had that day, "alone" didn't seem to be in their number.

"Bullshit," said his wise and wonderful mother sagely. "You are a good catch. You're smart, cute, funny, kind, a hard worker, an A student, and you laugh at my jokes. Out there someplace is a smart girl who will appreciate all of these fine qualities and decide she deserves to have you take her out. You don't have to tell her you laugh at my jokes until like the third or fourth date, it'll be fine."

A discussion ensued, liberally peppered with contributions by the siblings, about what kind of girl might find herself attracted to their brother.

"Human," said Mari, getting to the crux of the matter right from the start.

"Female."

"Ooh, and blonde."

"Or brunette."

"Or redhead!"

"Or just with some kind of hair."

"Pretty?" asked Jayce hopefully.

"Meh…" said all three siblings in unison.

Thus began one of many endlessly diverting family conferences on the topic of What Jayce Should Look For In A Girlfriend. This is one of those topics that is rehashed over and over, partially because the other kids can't resist the chance to tease their brother and partially because it tends to get sillier and sillier every time it comes up.

"She has to like trans people," Mari piped up loyally.

"And ostriches," said Gabi.

The room went quiet as the rest of us pondered where the hell ostriches entered into the deal.

"Ostriches?" Kaiden wanted to know. "What do ostriches have to do with anything?"

Gabi didn't know, she just knew ostriches were essential.

Mari, of all people, was able to clear up the mystery for us. "Jayce asked Gabi's Magic 8 Ball whether he should buy an ostrich and it said yes and now he's not allowed to use it anymore."

People stood around musing about what life at Casa Price would be like if Jayce actually purchased an ostrich. The truly scary thing was that nobody was quite able to say with conviction "Nah, he wouldn't do that…" because we were all pretty sure that, if the deal was good enough, he just might.

"Okay, so she has to like ostriches!" I said brightly. "I know how we tell if a girl is a blonde or not, but the ostrich question seems a little bit harder to get to in casual first date conversation."

"Well, she might have a shirt with an ostrich on it," said Gabi.

"Or a stuffed ostrich," Kaiden added. "Or an ostrich tattoo."

"Okay," I said, "so we're looking for a human female with some kind of hair and an ostrich tattoo who shows up to a date wearing an ostrich shirt and carrying an ostrich stuffed animal, but she can't be a whackjob."

Everyone except Jayce agreed that this was in fact the ideal woman for him. He wasn't certain. He had a nagging question.

"How does one go about opening up a potential romantic dialogue with this individual?" he wanted to know. "Let alone determining if she's a whackjob. And if things actually work out and she likes me, then what?"

"Ostrich love poetry!" I jumped up and down and clapped a little. I was pleased with myself. Sadly, I was about to be dealt a blow that would sound the death knell for this idea, dooming us to an existence forever bereft of the radiant imaginary daughter-in-law I already felt so close to. No doting father would walk her down the aisle in her wedding gown festooned with flightless African birds made out of organza and raw silk and hand her off to my beaming, slightly tearful son. There would be no release of homing ostriches to symbolize the beauty and purity of their love as they raced erratically over the flower-decked grounds, smashing rare heirloom marigolds to pulp beneath huge saurian feet.

"Mom, nothing rhymes with 'Ostrich.'"

Stymied by the limitations of the language of love, we were forced to acknowledge that not one of us could think of a good rhyme. In fact, if anyone reading this book thinks of especially poetic rhymes for the word, send them to Jayce in care of the publisher. He might just be able to put them to good use.

Settling for some other avian creature to rhyme with was unanimously deemed unacceptable, even one so obviously appropriate to wedding décor as the flamingo or so stately as the eagle. I decided to soldier forward.

"Poetry doesn't have to rhyme," I reminded them all. "And besides, if we do want it to rhyme, it is perfectly acceptable to use a rhyme that's not quite perfect but close." This is when inspiration struck.

"BOSTITCH!" I cried out. Then I stopped and looked to make sure the windows were closed, just in case some neighbor might be walking past and hear me holler "BOSTITCH!" and decide a 72-hour psychiatric hold was finally in order. Then I did it again. "BOSTITCH! Even better, Bostitch makes fasteners! This totally works, because a couple in love is FASTENED together!" I envisioned a stack of carefully kept love letters tied with a ribbon, with cute things in them like "I find you riveting" and "Your love is a staple in my life." My daughter-in-law was back, people! I was elated. Also yelling "BOSTITCH!" is oddly satisfying. Try it. I'll wait. Check your windows first.

Jayce: Not Sure About Ever Letting My Wife Meet My Mother. They'll End Up In Cahoots.

If you're transgender you might have the (mistaken, my mom says) belief that you're just going to die alone. It's easy to believe that nobody is going to want you because you're different. Sometimes you feel like no one will ever want you because you think of yourself as someone who will never be good enough if you weren't born with a body and a brain that match.

When I was growing up, I was supposed to be a perfect Jewish princess. And I was supposed to marry a Jewish man and be happy about it and he was supposed to be a lawyer. My former mother had this vision of me in a white lacy wedding dress, crying and joyful when I was proposed to. It was all this bullshit. It turns out I want to be the one proposing, and I want to be the one telling my family "Hey, I found a girl, and she is beautiful and she is 6'3" so I need somebody to follow me around with a stool just so I can kiss her."

Anyway, one day I was convinced I would never get married, never have kids, never have a family. My mom, who has gotten kids in literally every way possible, said "That's crap. If you want to be a husband you will be, and if you want to be a dad you will be."

So we started talking about what I should look for in a girlfriend. I want someone intelligent, someone I can laugh with and talk to, I want to feel safe and considered, someone that really has a sense of humor and understands me and all these good things, but I also kind of want all that stuff with someone who is pretty.

The truth is, she'll be the most beautiful woman in the world in my eyes if she connects with me that way. As a guy in his early 20s I'm just looking for someone female...

We were just throwing ideas around, and somehow or other Gabi remembered the Ostrich 8-Ball Disaster of 2018. I had shaken the thing up and said, "Oh Most Magical 8 Ball, should I buy an ostrich?" and the 8 ball said yes, so now I have a thing for ostriches and I'm not allowed to use the 8 ball anymore.

This means part of the dating questionnaire for any prospective romance has to include getting her opinions on ostriches. I figure it's good as an icebreaker.

I'm a songwriter, and I am pretty sure the ostrich related love song will be the best love song of the century.

I'm really just hoping to find someone who will love me for me. If you're trans you probably think this will never happen, but I know many trans people who are happily engaged and happily married and what it comes down to is that I should just stop thinking I'm gonna die alone and listen to my mother because she's always right.

Chapter 26

Kelly: Pronoun Trouble

Folks of a certain age remember Saturday mornings sitting in front of the TV set watching cartoons. In an effort to make our parents (who largely didn't care what we watched so long as we didn't bother them too much) happy, ABC ran this little series of cartoons in between the other cartoons that were designed to educate us even though it was Saturday. The series was called Schoolhouse Rock, and among the 64 episodes that aired starting in 1973 are some true classics that most Americans who were seventies era kids can sing. "I'm Just A Bill," "Interjections!" and "Conjunction Junction" taught kids about legislative processes, exclamation points, and little boxcars labeled "AND," "BUT," and "OR" respectively.

Among them was one about a guy named Albert Andreas Armadillo who was a friend of, but no relation to, a couple of kids named Rufus Xavier Sarsaparilla and Rafaela Gabriela Sarsaparilla.

Rufus Xavier Sarsaparilla had a kangaroo, Rafaela Gabriela Sarsaparilla had an aardvark, and Albert Andreas Armadillo had a rhinoceros. The aardvark adored Rafaela Gabriela Sarsaparilla, the kangaroo followed Rufus Xavier Sarsaparilla around as though Rufus Xavier had a continuous supply of RooSnaps Kangaroo Treats, and Albert Andreas Armadillo was so enamored of the rhinoceros that he routinely took it on public transportation.

Maybe you found the previous paragraph a little tiring. Maybe by the time you got to the end, you no longer gave a crap which character with what lengthy convoluted name had which weird pet. Maybe reading all those nouns over and over really wore you down. Well, my short-attention-span-afflicted American friends, I have wonderful news, because there are these cool words that are absolutely perfect for taking the places of all those nouns. Yes, that's right, I am talking about pronouns!! Cute handy little words like "he" and "she" and "I" and "you".

One problem exists, though.

Back in the day when A.A.A. and his R. rode the bus with R.G.S and R.X.S. and their A. and K. pets, pronouns were easier, because at that time *gender* was easier. According to society, if somebody had female anatomy, the correct pronouns were feminine, meaning she/her/hers. If someone had male anatomy, masculine pronouns were used, meaning he/him/his. There were some others, but pronouns were generally divided into two gender categories. If you wanted to talk about the lumberjackish sort of person next door and that person had been identified by society as female, you'd say "Wow, *she* really chopped down that tree fast, *she* is a tomboy!" Ditto the nice person next door on the other side with the prize-winning dahlias and the poodle with the rhinestone collar—that person was forever a *he*, and *his* dog was very cute and *his* flowers smelled heavenly when the wind was right. This was because *he* had been assigned as male by society.

Fast forward a couple of decades, and now there are kids all over the place running around thinking that instead of society telling them they're male or female based on how they look or act or the things they enjoy, they'd like to make those determinations for themselves. Also, a goodly number of them don't really feel particularly masculine OR particularly feminine. They might feel one way one day and another the next, or tend to stick someplace in the middle between the two "established" genders, or they might decide the whole concept of gender is complete rubbish and do away with entirely. Such people have always existed. Gender stereotypes are arbitrary, superficial, and changeable. Our current crop of kids is rebelling against being pigeonholed into using the pronouns they consider archaic and limiting.

About nine months into this adventure I got an inkling that Kaiden, who we'd thought was a girl, wanted to use a different name and pronouns. I got this idea from Jayce, who came to see me and said, "Did you know Kaiden wants a different name and pronouns?" He's sneaky like that. So I went to see Kaiden, who we'd thought was a girl, and said, "Do you need a different name and pronouns?" and he said, "Yes please, I'd like to be called Kaiden and I'm a 'he' please."

I responded to this revelation by going "Okay. I'm gonna mess up a lot, but I'm cool with it. What's your middle name gonna be?"

He didn't know yet. Had been thinking but hadn't found anything he really liked, but said he wanted it to begin with L so he could keep the same initials.

You're 26 chapters into this story now, so you can likely guess what happened next, and that is that every member of the household started yelling out suggestions.

"Lasagna!"

"Lutefisk!"

"Lollipop!"

"LOOOOOOOOON!"

I like that last one. I would work with "Kaiden Loon" any day. I get a lift when I just read the name.

For a lot of moms of trans kids who want to change their names, that is the hardest part. We choose baby names with great care, looking through books for a perfect name for hours and days and months. We try out initials, debate the name ideas with trusted close friends—the ones we can trust not to go "Ewww!" but who will still place a hand on our shoulders and say gently "Sweetie, in this day and age you just cannot name your child Boldemort, not even if that WAS your grandfather's name." For me, it was (and is) pronoun trouble.

Added to this was the revelation that Mari also would like to use "they/them/their" for pronouns, and my life has recently become a brain twisting mélange of different kids with different names and different pronouns. It is a well-known fact that when a mom has four kids she tends to go "Ja-Ka-Ga-Ma-DOG, come get your lunch!" We end up sounding like a small motor with a fuel mixture problem, and this is without trying to remember who's a he and who's a she and who's a they. The result is that you mess it up. All. The. Time.

"I wasn't calling you, I was calling your sis... sibling. She—they have their damn headphones on again."

"Price girls... crap... kids... get in the car already, we're late!"

Then you start calling the kid with the standard pronouns by "they" and have to correct it back the other way when the kid goes "Mom. I am a GIRL, you know."

After a few hours of this I begin to get a tad peevish and fatigued, and I begin to sprinkle my conversations with epithets, causing the corrected pronoun "They" and the epithet "Fuck" to blend together to become "Theyfuck." If the younger kids are around I modulate it to "Theycrap" but the basic idea is the same. This tendency is exaggerated when upon receiving a request for some simple thing, such as "Tell Mari I said to come wipe the bananas off the cat! She left a huge mess!" you hear not the expected responses of "Why should I, I haven't put bananas on the cat in years, those are not my bananas..." and "It's Gabi's turn!" Instead all four children yell from different parts of the house "THEY, Mom!"

I invariably repeat my request at a slightly higher volume, and the kids respond in typical child fashion. These sweet angels whose little shell-like ears were deft enough to identify single syllable pronoun errors through two closed doors and a set of Skullcandy knockoff ear buds—will answer by going "HUH???"

Jayce: Just Respect The Damn Pronouns

Some people may think that the subject of pronouns is difficult, sensitive or complicated. The truth is, is it isn't at all. My name is Jayce, I am male and my pronouns are he/him/his. It's not hard. When I first told my ex-father who I was, he said "hey kiddo, this is too political". It's not political at all, it's just basic respect, and even if the idea of respecting people's pronouns crosses into political territory, why should that change anything? You're talking with an individual, not a political organization. If someone says my pronouns are he, or they, or she, fine. You say "okay" and move on. You don't have to understand it because it isn't about you. Hell, I don't always understand it myself.

Misgendering happens in the world, a lot. But there's a difference between forgetting, messing up, apologizing, and correcting it, versus misgendering to attack. For me, my ex-parents called me she, or they and there's nothing that felt worse at that moment because they didn't care that they were hurting me. Before my transition having someone call me "she" made me feel just awful, sick and sad and not valued or validated.

Since I transitioned, it doesn't really affect me anymore if someone misgenders me because it can happen to anyone, trans or not. Sometimes I'll correct them. Sometimes I won't because it doesn't matter to me all that much anymore. Some people are really sensitive and triggered by it, but I find that once you are more comfortable with yourself and know who you are, it won't spin you nearly as much.

So my advice to you, if someone tells you their name and pronouns, just go with it because it costs you nothing and means everything to them. They are giving you a piece of their identity, respect that confidence and care for them.

Chapter 27
Kelly: Road Trips, Ferris Wheels, And The Cycle Of Bullshit

In the course of a typical American childhood, the call of the highway sometimes becomes too much to resist. Summer just doesn't quite feel like summer without a road trip. The pull of rolling hills and panoramic views and togetherness causes a crazy kind of amnesia in which all of the memories of previous trips are magically erased. Families pile into vehicles with suitcases and toys and lots of snacks and proceed to get bored in 4.1 seconds and start hollering "Are we there yet? How many miles? I need to go to the bathroom! Hey, can we stop, I see a video arcade! When's lunch? Can I eat these gummy bears I found in the seat? I think I left my shoe at the last rest stop, we have to go back! I feel like I'm gonna barf..."

This litany goes on for the entire time the family is in the vehicle unless, that is, the children are eating junk food. This makes it imperative that lots and lots of snacks be procured for any trip longer than ninety minutes. Lucky Charms, spray cheese in a can, Red Vines, an endless supply of Jolly Ranchers, and chips make up the majority of the road tripping child's travel diet. Nomadic tribes from past centuries fed their children nutritious pemmican supplemented with wild vegetables and freshly hunted meat. We grab a bag of pork rinds and get back in the car to play leapfrog with semis for eight or nine hours.

The Price clan set off last summer for Minnesota, to attend a family reunion planned by Daniel's uncle on his mom's side of the family. This is a very large family. Daniel's mother was one of nine kids, and now those kids have kids and grandkids and in one case great-grandkids, and so when we get together there are a hell of a lot of us. It was the first time Jayce would be meeting that part of the family, and he was a little bit nervous. Or, possibly, a lot nervous. We had plans on a different day to spend time with Daniel's father's side of the family as well, and this made for a lot of introductions to a lot of people in a very short time. There was also, of course, the question of Who Knows Jayce Is Trans, because that question is always someplace at the forefront of a trans kid's mind when social occasions happen. The vast majority of Daniel's family are very accepting people who have a talent for recognizing that nobody's perfect and that people are what they are.

"The people who know are the people who were gonna know anyway," I told him. "Pretty much if they're on Facebook with me, they know. Nobody's gonna be mean to you, and if they are I'll get up in their faces about it." He shot me a skeptical look and made a sort of muttering noise of disbelief.

I myself was looking forward to the trip partially because I felt the need to have a brief meeting with the uncle responsible for creating and maintaining the family tree. A couple of years back, at the previous family reunion, I discovered that this particular uncle had left Gabi and Mari off of the family tree document. When I questioned him about this he had informed me casually "Oh, they're not on there, they're not blood relatives."

I went speechless. This is not my default state, as the reader can likely surmise by now. I kind of went "B-b-b-b..." and then walked away to go complain to Daniel's cousin Angie, who is awesome and who was equally appalled. Family is family, and it doesn't matter how somebody got there, all that matters is that they are there and they're loved. Anyway, word filtered through the clan and so this year the same uncle showed up with a bunch of paperwork and wanted everyone to make sure their family info was correct and up to date. I completed my form very carefully, and I added Jayce Kennedy Price as well.

"Well," Uncle Family Tree told me while we waited in the food line, "we're gonna put them on there, but they have to have an asterisk and some indication that they're adopted, not blood, and therefore not really related to us."

"Well," I responded in the same conversational tone, "based on that definition I'm not really related to you either, so if you're not gonna put them ON then go ahead and take me OFF."

Eventually he gave up talking to me, flapped his hands in an exasperated way, and wandered off. I counted this as a victory.

The reunion was highly successful. Jayce got to meet everyone and play basketball with an aunt and a couple of cousins. I got my ass kicked at badminton again, having driven the badminton set across most of Nebraska for the purpose. Gabi got to play Jenga with her cousin, the engineer. Mari and the great-grandkids clambered all over the play structures. Kaiden moved from place to place and read a book, which is Kaiden's way of being social. The rest of the trip included jet ski rides, kayaking, riding on the tube behind the jet ski (I did not know I could scream that loud), swimming, and other typical Lake Vacation pursuits. On the way home we stayed at a farmhouse I found on AirBnB that was absolutely lovely, with green grass and flowers all around it and millions of little Viceroy butterflies like orange jewels in the air. You could stir up clouds of them when you walked across the grounds.

Near that stop was an old-fashioned county fair complete with animals, quilt and jam displays, and midway rides. Each child started clamoring for a ride on one of the ancient clanking machines that littered the grounds, and we blew enough money on tickets to let each person do one ride. Most of the crew wanted to do the Ferris wheel, as it is a relatively benign gadget without a whole lot of G-forces.

"I hate Ferris wheels, Mom." Jayce swallowed hard and eyeballed the gargantuan wheel. "People always rock the seats. I hate them. I don't wanna go on there." He kept looking at the thing awhile. I could see wheels turning in his mind as he vacillated between thinking "Son of a bitch, I can't ride a Ferris wheel, I am a weenie" and "I am not going on that thing."

The desire to avoid weeniehood won the day, but only if he got to ride with me. "I wanna go with Mom," he told Kaiden and Mari, who agreed to this plan with cheerful alacrity.

We were eventually allowed to board by a surly fellow with no teeth whose drug screen results would have been questionable at best, and off we went, whoosh, to the top.

I sat perfectly still. No rocking whatsoever occurred. Jayce looked out over the fields and said, "I don't like being up here, Mom."

"Jayce. Look around you. It's green. You can see the whole state of Nebraska from up here. It's the Cycle of Bullshit. The sun warms the earth and causes plants to photosynthesize and then the plants feed the bull and the bull enriches the earth. It's a great cosmic dance. Like the food web, except it's the Bullshit Web."

By this time he was laughing, despite being fifty feet in the air.

"How did I get along for eighteen years without you, Mom?" he wondered aloud. I said I didn't know either, and the ride came back to the bullshit-rich earth, and we disembarked and headed off in search of sustenance in the form of pie.

They had a bunch of buildings on the fairgrounds that had picnic tables outside of them. Each building was being manned—or womanned, in many cases—by a gang of people from the different churches in town. They sold the sort of homemade pie that people who are nostalgic about pie remember their grandmothers making. Fresh raspberries and strawberries, rhubarb, nuts, and a lot of love went into those pies. There seemed to be a rather intense Pie Rivalry happening, and I conjured up a visual in my head of a lot of women in flowered housedresses brandishing rolling pins and reenacting the Rumble scene from *West Side Story*. After some careful thought that took into account variables like crust flakiness and the effort we believed went into the pies, we went to the Catholic Pie building (nine flavors!) and ate a lot of pie. Then we headed back to the farmhouse for a search for fireflies and bedtime.

That road trip was hands down the best summer road trip I have ever done. It was the quintessential American experience everyone hopes for when they plan one of these things. Everybody got along pretty well most of the time, we had plenty of unstructured time to play, and the weather was absolutely perfect until we hit a really epic summer thunderstorm a hundred miles from home and had to pull over on the interstate. One night when we were all crammed into a hotel room in Minneapolis I got up to visit the bathroom in the darkness and I was reflecting on how the room was littered with the people I love most in the whole world, and I went back to bed in a state of absolute contentment.

Jayce agrees with me about this. His previous experiences with family vacations tended to be pretty traumatic, so going on a normal vacation where the most horrible thing that happened was me screaming my head off on a tube behind a jet ski was something of a revelation for him. He kept shaking his head and going "Wow. This is weird. It's normal, which is weird. It's weirdly normal. Or normally weird. Weird."

247

Jayce: Reclaiming the Roadtrip

Growing up, I absolutely despised family vacations. They were awful. I'd have to travel to Florida maybe 3-4 times a year to visit my grandparents, and so I was completely sick of Florida. Every time I would try to be optimistic and think "Okay this is gonna be a good trip," and then after about a day it always turned out I was wrong. Everybody always blamed everything on me, like I just could not be well-behaved. I felt like a bomb about to go off most of the time.

I would find myself in fistfights with my father that he started, I would get punished for the most ridiculous things and screamed at, and nobody could ever get along. It always seemed to be two against one, whether that was my parents against me, me and my father against my mom, or mom and I against my dad. I can't remember a single good vacation I ever had with them.

One time we were in a different state, and I was younger, like 9 or 10. They wanted to drag me to a very boring plantation, and I didn't want to go. I went anyway because I had no choice.

They were mad at me for something, I can't recall what. They screamed at me and made me get out of the car and then they just drove off and left! There was nobody there. I was all alone on this deserted plantation and of course I didn't have a phone, and there was nobody around for miles and I genuinely thought they had left me forever. I was hysterically crying because they drove off, I couldn't see them, I had no idea when or if they were coming back, and I was 9 or 10 years old. I thought I had lost my parents.

About an hour later they came back. Apparently my father had said "We can't just leave her permanently." I'm like "Oh wow, thank you for that…" It was just an awful, awful vacation. I dreaded vacations.

In July of 2019 I got to take my first family vacation with the Prices in the summertime. We went to a family reunion for Daniel's mom's family. Daniel has a big family and I was nervous about meeting all these people, because I'd lived 19 years of my life and I didn't know my relatives. In my former family I didn't know them either, I only met them when we went to funerals and such. Other than that, I didn't really know anybody.

I was kind of shy for a while and on edge, thinking "What am I even doing here?" I'm a social person, but there were over fifty people there and it was a lot for me. It just took a lot of energy out of me. A lot of these people didn't even know who I was, some didn't know how I got here, but most of them were very accepting.

Once the big reunion was over and we got back to a smaller crowd, I got to meet some people on my dad's father's side of the family, and I had some of the best times I ever had in the summer in my life. My dad and I found something to do together and went to a Minnesota Twins baseball game. I have always enjoyed watching baseball, but this was the best baseball game I have ever been to. Some of his relatives were there and I got to meet them, and I liked them. The game was in the ninth inning, and the score was tied with two outs, and one of the Minnesota Twins hitters hit a walk-off home run and ended up putting the score over the top. My dad was texting my mom "Well, we're about to go into extra innings… wait never mind!" It was the best baseball game I've ever been to because I got to share it with people I actually liked. That was a new experience for me.

The next day we hung out with these people more, and I had the best day at the lake that I have EVER had. The whole day was just amazing. There was no screaming, no hitting, no one was telling me I was doing anything stupidly wrong. It was just a really fun day. I got to learn to ride a jet ski, and we went tubing, and I absolutely loved it but my mom learned that she is never doing it again because Daniel's uncle is in his seventies and he has a need for speed. He likes to crank the jet ski up to seventy miles an hour and then complains that it's too slow. I just felt like me, I felt like a guy hanging out on the lake all day and just having a ton of fun. So overall our trip was really normal, and I felt like I got to reclaim a special part of what childhood should be.

On the way back home we stopped in Nebraska, and I got to go to a real county fair. I had never gotten to do anything like this. I had never seen cattle up close and pigs and huge bunnies in cages and just eat pie that was made by local church ladies and watch BMX bikers do tricks. It was a childhood experience I had never gotten to have, and I think my parents were hoping for that. Then we went on the Ferris wheel.

I've been on a few roller coasters, but I've never been much of an adrenaline junkie. I never went on Ferris wheels. My former mother would always scare me, and rock the chair back and forth and make me feel like I was gonna fall. Of course, there was trauma related to everything.

My mom and I got on the Ferris wheel, and of course I was holding onto the bar for dear life, and as you know we use humor to get me out of scared traumatized states. My mom started babbling about the cycle of bullshit, and of course we got laughing so hard I forgot what I was scared about.

The worst thing we had happen on the whole trip was people arguing in the car about whose turn it was to use the charger. No one screamed at me, no one hit me, and no one even abandoned me on the side of the road. It was a good time.

Chapter 28

Kelly: Jayce Kennedy and the Terrible, Horrible, No Good, Very Bad Day

Jayce set a specific goal for himself for fall semester at school. He thought things over carefully, came to find me one day, and said "Mom, I am going to plan to have a bullshit free semester. This semester will have much less bullshit. I am going to make sure of it."

Little did he know that something in the universe that has a sense of humor and loves proving people wrong was listening.

Before we left on the road trip, Jayce had managed to get into a fender bender involving a lane change, a rear end collision, and a decision about stopping for a yellow light rather than just plowing through it. Accounts of who did what when in this accident diverged in terms of who was at fault, but the upshot in the end was that Jayce got the ticket—and thus the liability—for the crash. This included a mandatory court hearing on a Monday morning. We expressed our gratitude that nobody was seriously injured and got on with things. When we got home, Jayce took his car in to be repaired and while that was happening the insurance company gave him a rental car to drive.

"You're under 25," the rental agent told him, "so we can't offer you the loss/damage waiver plan on the rental car."

I reflected that the under 25 demographic was very likely the group who needed the loss/damage waiver plan most, but said what the hell, my hands were tied, and we rented him a little black Elantra.

He was incredibly anxious about the court appearance.

"They're gonna put me in jail, Mom," he said the night before.

"No, kiddo, they don't jail people for fender benders. At least not unless the people in question are breaking the law in some other way, like carrying random human body parts or having their fender bender in a stolen car." He remained uncertain despite my reassurances, convinced that the best he could hope for was a quick body cavity search and a low bail figure.

The day of his scheduled court hearing arrived, and he went off to the courthouse to be processed along with all the other miscreants on the docket that day. I rearranged my schedule so I could go along for moral support, and he put on some decent clothes so he'd look like he gave a damn, and we headed over to City Hall. Jayce got a nice lady judge who offered him a plea bargain deal, which he was intelligent enough to accept once he understood why that was happening. His bank account took a hit, but not a really big hit.

"Hey Mom, my credit card only screamed a little bit!" he told me later.

Pleased and relieved, he headed off to take the rental car back. You know, the little Elantra with no loss/damage waiver on it? That was more foreshadowing I did back there. I'm telling you this now because you needed to pay attention and I want to make sure you don't miss the important bits.

Jayce got within two blocks of the rental return office, turned onto a freeway onramp for some reason I never did figure out, and was sideswiped and nearly squished by a McDonalds truck. The side of the trailer climbed over the passenger side of the Elantra and made a long straight dent in the window and tore the mirror completely off. I didn't know it was possible to dent glass, but apparently it is, because dented it definitely was.

My cell phone rang.

"MOMMMM, you are not going to believe this, I got hit by a fucking semi." He was clearly conscious, so I didn't panic.

"Whoa," I said. "Slow down. Anybody hurt?"

"NOOOOO," he said, "But I am really pissed off. This was definitely not my fault! I was in my own lane!"

His speech then devolved briefly into an incoherent but creatively profane rant that resulted in my taking him off the Bluetooth in my van so the littler kids didn't learn more new naughty words. I waited for him to pause to breathe and asked, "Where are you?"

"I don't know! How should I know? I'm on a goddamn road!"

I made a deductive effort worthy of Sherlock Holmes and was eventually able to figure out roughly where he was.

"Hang on," I told the little kids. "We gotta go rescue your brother. He got in a wreck."

"AGAIN??!!" they hollered from the back of the van. "Are you freaking kidding?" Various frustrated growling noises ensued when I confirmed this. They wanted to go home and play video games. They did not want to deal with any more crap that day. They were contemplating mutiny.

I quelled the incipient riot with a gimlet stare and "Do you think your brother drove under a semi on purpose?" They conceded that he (probably) had not, and we started down the road.

A few minutes later we got to the accident scene and were greeted by two cops, one very irritated truck driver, and an extremely upset Jayce. I told the little kids not to get out of the car for any reason and joined them all on the ramp.

The police officers involved, a man and a lady from the city of Wheatridge, were doing their best to figure out what exactly had gone wrong.

"I've been driving thirty-five years!" the trucker ranted. "How old are you? Like fifteen? Do you even have a license?" This was a bittersweet moment for Jayce, who had just been in another car crash and who was a little bit shaken and stressed. Plus he looks about fifteen at this point in his second puberty. The good part though was that he got to hand over a driver's license *with his chosen name on it*. Really, there would be nothing that would make a transgender kid's day more complete than having to out himself to some cop on a freeway onramp because the driver's license name doesn't match the appearance. There is also the issue of discrimination, which is an ongoing and pervasive fact of life for trans people.

Here is an opportunity for a children's book, so I hope Laura Numeroff reads this. If you give a cop a license, he's gonna want a photo to go with it. If you give him the photo, he'll remember that people with girl names don't usually act or look so much like boys and he'll ask you an invasive question. If you answer the question, he'll ask five more invasive questions. You'll have to answer those too. Then he'll remember that he knows somebody else who is trans. He'll want to decorate your record with police reports in a variety of fonts. You'll have to empty your bank account. Then you will work a lot of overtime at menial jobs. You'll eventually want to open a new bank account. And chances are, when you open your new bank account, they're gonna want to see a license.

The police verified all of Jayce's identifying information, wandered over the accident scene, talked to a couple of drivers who stopped as witnesses, and ultimately decided that the incident was the result of driver inexperience and turning radii of tractor trailers. They asked that we get everyone off the freeway onramp. I looked at my kid, who was shaking and running his hands through his hair and repeating himself a lot ("The same day. As court. The. Same. DAY. The same fucking day!") and I drew the conclusion that he really should not drive just yet and went to ask the police if we could leave the rental car in the weeds off the onramp while I took the kids for some lunch.

"It's just bullshit," I told Jayce over lunch at Burger King. Normally they might have chosen McDonald's, but as everyone was angry with the entire McDonald's corporation for sending a guy in a truck to squish my boy child, we ended up at Burger King.

"It's just bullshit! Nobody was hurt, the rental car is driveable to the drop off place, we'll file (another) insurance claim and pay the deductible and your rates will go up and it's just bullshit. We know how to deal with bullshit."

Eventually he got most of a Whopper inside him and we headed back to the scene and picked up the rental car and he managed to drive it over to the rental office, where they were very kind and said "Oh, this isn't that bad, you should see some of the ones people bring back in, half the time I can't figure out how they get them here." He paid the deductible, causing his credit card to scream a little louder, and then he decided to go to the pool for a relaxing swim.

"Don't drown," I told him.

The little kids and I went home and I got into the bath, because soaking in the tub and reading escapist trash is one of my favorite ways of coping with stress, and half an hour later the phone rang again.

For most purposes, my phone ringtone is one taken from a YouTube video of this brilliant lunatic named Franco Munoz who can play music on rubber chickens. I selected "Despacito Chicken," and it rarely fails to entertain me when it rings.

Jayce has his own ringtone, however. His is the Harry Potter theme song, played on piano, and by this time I was starting to get a little bit punchy when I heard it. So when it rang again one of my eyelids started to twitch a little bit and I crawled wistfully out of the tub to answer it.

"Mom, you are not going to believe this one," he told me, greatly underestimating my capacity to believe nearly anything he could throw at me. "I went to jump in the pool and felt this awful pain and my leg is killing me and I didn't drown." I couldn't quite tell whether he was laughing or crying at this point, and our cell service here blows so he kept cutting out, further confusing the issue.

"Well shit," I said. "I'll be up in a second." I got dressed and told the little kids to sit there and play video games and not move, and they didn't even look up, they just said, "Uh huh…" and sank beneath the surface of Video Game World without a ripple.

It was true that Jayce had followed my instructions and not drowned. I probably should have issued a more general edict along the lines of "Don't hurt yourself," though, because he could not bear weight on his right leg at all. I ran my hands over it searching for signs of a fracture and didn't find anything, but the fact remained that the boy could not walk without significant pain. He said he hadn't hit anything or landed wrong, either, just jumped in the pool, swore really loudly, and crawled back out again.

We loaded the little kids back in the car and went to the ER. X-rays didn't show a break, which was good, and they put him in a splint, gave him a pair of crutches and a brief lesson on how to use them, and sent him home.

Our local fire department has this brilliant thing set up that is called Dave's Locker. Dave decided that the community needed a sort of library for medical equipment like shower chairs and knee scooters and such, and so if you're not anticipating needing these things long term you can go see Dave and borrow them, and that is what I did. Jayce of course flatly refused to use the knee scooter unless it was dark outside because he said, "it looks dorky." Which I grant you it definitely did, but Emma Watson wasn't scheduled to stop by any time soon so I wasn't too worried about it. The shower chair, though, was destined to come in handy, and here we come to another of those places where life's occurrences are colored by the implications of someone being transgender.

Way back in about November of last year Jayce decided to cook some potato pancakes for the family, a decision that made Mari very happy as they adore potato pancakes. While shredding the potatoes Jayce managed to amputate the very tip of his thumb with my mandoline. If you don't cook much, a mandoline is this absolutely deadly little bladed apparatus that you can use for making very thin uniform slices of things like potatoes or onions. Mandolines hunger for blood like something you'd buy from the Pampered Vampire Chef catalog. It is completely unrelated to a musical mandolin, although I suppose you could whack it with a spoon and make sort of a percussion thing out of it.

Anyhow, that was our first trip to the emergency room together, and it was just good fortune that the day before I had noted the ER location and that they accepted Jayce's insurance and so all was well... until he realized that he'd need help taking off his binder. These things cannot be removed without the use of both thumbs. There are YouTube videos that are devoted solely to teaching trans people how to remove a binder. Most trans guys get irrevocably stuck in binders at least once. Following this particular incident Jayce had to tolerate having me assist him with this process. I shut my eyes and we got it done, but you can imagine his joy.

The leg injury situation wasn't a whole lot different. He had to have the splint encased firmly in garbage bags so as not to get it wet, then he had to have assistance in the bathroom in the form of me handing him things while he showered and then while he got dressed. I kept my eyes tightly shut the entire time and he was able to get clean without wrecking the splint, compromising his dignity (much), or becoming too dysphoric or triggered.

Later, we were reflecting on the day in Jayce's bedroom. "This is not the worst day I've ever had, Mom," he told me, "but it's in the top five."

The other four must have been pretty spectacularly bad. I decided I really didn't want to know, said goodnight, and left the crutches in reach.

Jayce: A Lotta Bullshit

They say the road to Hell is paved with good intentions. I was intending to enter my sophomore year in college in an uncomplicated way. I really wanted life to look less nuts and more normal, but apparently I don't know how to do this.

Getting blamed for that car accident really pissed me off. The guy behind me was apparently thinking I would go through the yellow light and so he just didn't stop. He bashed into me, and I got the ticket anyway, which seemed totally unfair. My mom calls that the "BS Teenage Tax."

I was in shock and shaken up and didn't know what to do, so I called my mom and said, "How are you, by the way, I got in a car crash." I think she was in Loveland, I'm not sure, but she was somewhere far away, at the Colorado Renaissance Festival. Anyway, she had to come rescue me because of course the first thing I'd done was lock my keys in the car. I was so shocked and shaken up. The cop insisted I call a tow truck but Mom showed up just in time to get me out of paying for that.

Since I got stuck with the ticket, I was convinced I would end up going to jail. Mom said that they don't put you in jail for a fender bender. I didn't believe her and I ended up waiting for the court date and being very scared. I thought it would be worse than it was, but I was pleasantly surprised to discover the existence of something called a plea bargain, and when the lawyer explained it to me it turned out I could actually afford the fine.

While my car was being checked over, I had a rental car that was covered by my auto insurance. The next day, I had to return the rental car. I was about two blocks away from the rental car place, on a highway onramp. I was in a double left turn lane and a semi turned on top of me. I couldn't even get more than ¾ of the way through the turn before I was forced to drive out from underneath the truck. My rental car was already squashed under the truck. Luckily I wasn't injured. The police arrived and they said the fault was shared between the truck driver and I. They said we had both failed to "read the road" correctly and so nobody got a ticket. I was grateful for that part. It was also good to hand the officer my driver's license knowing that it said my correct name and gender.

We finally got to the rental car place with the bashed up car. I told the agent what had happened and ended up paying a $500 insurance deductible, which I actually had in the bank since the fine for the first accident had been so low, so that part was good.

So we left there and that was when I figured out I'd lost my bracelet. This was a bracelet with my new name on it, Jayce Kennedy Price, that had been given to me by the Kennedys themselves. It was a very important gift to me, and so my mom went back and she found it, so the day got better again.

I decided I was pretty lucky to have gotten out of the wreck unhurt. I needed to unwind, so I went swimming. I jumped in the pool like I have 1000 times, and I felt this terrible stabbing pain in my leg, and I couldn't figure out if I had broken it or what. At first I thought it was just a cramp, but it turns out if you're on T you're more prone to pulling muscles. So that was great.

I crawled out of the pool and called Mom, and over the phone she couldn't figure out if I was laughing or crying. Neither could I! She said, "What the hell did you do?" and I said, "I don't know, but I can't walk." I had no idea what was wrong, I just knew it hurt a lot, so she picked me up and then we went the two blocks back home and picked up the little kids. Mari just GROWLED at me, and I couldn't blame them.

We got to urgent care and my leg was swollen and painful. I was really hoping I hadn't torn my Achilles tendon, which luckily I hadn't, but I did pull a muscle. I ended up in a really sexy brace and got crutches and got to get around that way for a few days, and it was irritating as hell.

At the time Anna had broken her foot doing a thing in dance class that she had done a thousand times, but this time she rolled over her foot and broke it. Between us we had one pair of functioning legs but she injured her left and I injured my right and that meant she could at least drive and I could not.

I told Anna the story and she said "Wait, you hurt your leg AFTER the accident?"

I said, "Yeah, it's not what you would think, is it?"

This was not the first time she and I were recovering from similar injuries at the same time. The first wreck had given me a concussion, and she had also been recovering from a concussion sustained at dance, and so we had matching injuries more than once. Remember what I said about no bullshit? It turns out that was bullshit.

Chapter 29

Shit My Mom Says

Language constantly evolves in our society. Cultural references, memes, slang terms, brand names, current events, and Twitter quotes all contribute to our understanding of our world and culture in ways we rarely consider. A mansion is one thing, a McMansion is something completely different, but if you're from these parts you know exactly what that difference is without being told.

Song jingles work the same way. If I write the phrase "Oh, I wish I were an…" most of you are instantly going to sing the "Oscar Mayer wiener…" part. It's etched into our collective consciousness. Typing out "Meow meow meow meow" causes a bouncy little tune to appear in your head that just might keep you awake at night, primarily because the lyrics are so poetic and moving. It is the best song ever sung by a cat.

If you have a family, the odds are excellent that you also have a family lexicography. This is a series of words or terms that are coined by members of a group and used within that group, with all of the group members understanding exactly what is meant. A fair number of these come from inside jokes, which I happen to believe are a significant ingredient in the glue that holds a family together. Married people especially tend to develop a way of communicating things between themselves that they can use even in a crowd, ways to say, "My God this party is dull, can we please go home and watch the Muppet Show on DVD instead?"

A fair number of the terms in our personal family lexicography have come from kids, or people who were once kids. Around here everyone knows that if you ask for "Mokiki" for dinner you mean macaroni and cheese, and it better be the kind in the box with the day-glo orange powder crap. We have two cats named Nizel and Kabo because when Kaiden was small he had an imaginary friend named Nizel-Kabo who was a cat. Kaiden would call the imaginary cat on an imaginary cell phone and invite him to play in those unsanitary play Habitrails at McDonald's. Llamas are always going to be called Yamels by us because my sister Holly couldn't think of the word "llama" once. This has been a word we have used for something like forty-five years now. If you played it in Scrabble we would all go "Yup, that's a word" and give you the points for it without even hesitating.

Jayce's personality, like mine, is one that tends to see humor in literally everything, and as a result there have been a lot of inside jokes and new and dumb terms that have stemmed from our adventures together. Jayce and I met some of his old friends for lunch one day and they said they didn't understand half of what we were talking about because it was like we had our own complete language.

I am going to go ahead and brag for a minute here because I have made a bunch of colorful contributions to the Price family phrase book, and now here they are for your entertainment and edification. Or something.

Kelly: You Want Me To Go Away, Don't You?

Parenting this boy has required stubbornness and persistence on my part, and I frequently deploy one of my favorite parenting techniques ever when interacting with him. We call it "You want me to go away, don't you?" because that is exactly what I say – and do – in order to get him to do something I need him to do at a given moment. It is especially effective on teenagers, especially if you then start doing something really annoying in their rooms like touching all their stuff. If you have a teen, try this and watch the desperation in their eyes as you stand there in their personal space whistling a cheery little tune and sticking your fingers into their Lego creations or just picking things up at random and putting them back down in slightly different spots. You're not doing anything obnoxious, you're just, you know, hanging out. They get to the point where they will do just about anything in order to make you go away, including things like hauling a full basket of laundry upstairs or mowing the lawn.

This is another of those techniques that works really well when dealing with bureaucratic entities of the type that isn't quite as regimented as the Social Security office or the DMV. Say for example you show up to the desk at your friendly rental car company and they have messed up your reservation and are now telling you that the SUV they promised you is unavailable and that your family of six people will just have to make do with the Dodge Neon that IS available instead. It's really easy to just go completely ballistic and scream at somebody, but the odds are that your little tantrum will be unproductive in the extreme. Instead, your goal is to make SURE they want you to go away. You can therefore try asking them to look up your account online four times, conveniently remembering the password on the fourth try. You can ask to borrow a phone because yours is broken or has a low battery. You can engage in any activity that makes you appear polite but inept and delays them in the pursuit of their job. They'll want you to go away, and they'll offer to borrow an SUV from some other location just so you will do so.

Jayce: Accurate.

Everybody has their own ways of communicating with each other and expressing love in a family. One of the reasons my mom and I have always stayed so close is because we connect with humor. There is a bunch of things my mom says that are inside jokes, and whenever she says them we laugh and we know exactly what we're talking about.

All she has to do is say, "You want me to go away, don't you?" and I'll do anything she is asking me to do. Within reason, anyway. I do want her to go away. I don't want her to go away forever, but for her to go away temporarily until next time she has to bug me about something would be great. The thing about getting her to go away is that she always comes back. Laundry and cleaning the bro cave (my room) and writing papers without bitching are all things she uses this for. She *knows* I want her to go away, until the next time she appears, and she uses that to her advantage all the time. That's how she gets her way. It's like Parenting 101. In my former family people would scream and hit and take things away, and all Mom has to do is say "You want me to go away, don't you?" and I do what she wants. It's amazing.

Kelly: It's All About Me

This one involves spinning a situation so that it appears that whatever thing I have just done for (or to) a given child was done solely for my benefit. Variations on the theme include ideas like "Whatever you do to treat the dysphoria means I get more sleep, because it's all about me," and "We are going to the emergency room that's on the way to my job because it's all about me."

If you're a new mom and you're under the impression that it actually IS all about you, there is a disclaimer attached to this chapter, because no, it ain't, so sorry, bye.

Jayce: It's all about Mom

Another thing Mom likes to say is "It's all about me." It's funny because in my former family it really was all about them, and here we joke that it's all about mom, and how she has to get sleep and how we all deprive her of sleep, and how everything we do has some connection back to her. We all know really that everything she asks us to do is in our own best interest, but it is all about her so she can meet her goal of raising a bunch of well nourished, responsible, and educated, terrible criminals.

Kelly: Trans Chips

These are those spicy little rolled corn chips that are coated in bright red flavor powder. We started calling them Trans Chips one day when we were talking about environmental causes of gender dysphoria and Jayce was eating a bowl of them.

The way Jayce consumes these chips is one of the weirder things he does in a long list of weird things, and the first time I watched the process I did so with a kind of bemused wonder about the depth of his eccentricity. What he does is this: He takes a full bag of the chips and dumps them into a large bowl, smashes them to red powdery bits and then eats the powder in heaping spoonfuls. I made a dumb observation that maybe the concentrated powder was an environmental cause of his being transgender and that he should be careful about getting that stuff all over the house because it might be contagious. This evolved into an inane ritual in the grocery store that requires that we handle the bags of chips as though they were bombs about to go off and turn everybody trans.

"Whoa, dude, go slow with that, you wanna spread it through the whole store? Okay, now walk carefully, and for God's sake don't drop that bag!"

Eventually the bag of chips gets placed oh so carefully into the cart and we both wipe imaginary sweat from our brows and say, "That was a close one!" It has occurred to me to make t-shirts for us in pink, white, and blue that say "Transgender Bomb Squad" on them just to see if anyone would ask us questions about them.

At home I will occasionally steal one of the chips from the bag before he smashes them to smithereens.

"Mom," he will say. "Be careful with that, you might have natural immunity but you know what happens when you eat too many of those..."

"Yeah," I respond, "I wondered why I had a sudden desire to go lie under my van and swear a lot."

Jayce: They're delicious

Another joke we share is about 'trans chips'. I have been eating these things since like 2011, I am totally addicted to them. I never really thought they were the reason I was trans, but now every time we leave to go get stuff done we have to take these chips with us, just because it's funny. We're convinced that because I crush them into powder the floating bits must have gotten into the air and turned everyone else in the house trans.

Kelly: Trans Crap Tuesdays

The day of the week that Jayce ended up starting his testosterone shots is conveniently alliterative, because Trans Crap Friday just doesn't sound as good. We are all busy and scattered around here, and forgetting to do his weekly shot wouldn't be good for him, so in my phone and calendar I have reminder entries that say "Trans Crap Tuesday" followed by the number of weeks he's been on the shots. So "TCT #33" means that on Trans Crap Tuesday he's due for weekly shot number 33. Other parents of trans kids think we are nuts because we just don't feel a need to disguise the fact that he's got Trans Crap to do every week.

Tuesday mornings also used to be a favorite time for us to drive all over hell trying to deal with gender related bureaucracy because he was off school and I was off work. It was a good day to go argue with people at the DMV, make physician and therapy appointments, or deal with whatever stuff was up next on the Big Scary Checklist of Logistical Insanity.

Jayce: Trans and Tuesday both start with T

That brings us to "Trans Crap Tuesdays." Any bureaucratic errands or shots or anything else that has to do with trans ends up scheduled on Tuesdays. At first it was entirely coincidental, but now we have actually started trying to schedule things like this on Tuesdays.

Kelly: Get In The Box

There comes a point in the lives of most parents when, after following all of the instructions on good parenting by the Kid Instruction Manuals that people insist on creating, Mom and Dad resort to threats. We eventually just sort of crack after the five thousandth time of trying to explain to our sweet little goblins that if they don't put their shoes on we will be late for school and that being late for school is frowned upon in our society. Generally, the next statement will be something on the order of "If you don't get dressed for school THIS INSTANT I am gonna sell all your clothes and send you to school nude!" If you're that parent who is going to claim never to do this, buzz off, you are not my tribe, I can't even relate to your perfection. You probably never let your kids go out in plaid pants and a floral shirt, either. You are a droid.

Around here I am eternally telling my kids that if they don't do (insert task here) or stop doing (insert annoying, destructive, or dangerous behavior here) immediately, I am going to box them up and FedEx them to Timbuktu. It's always Timbuktu, I have no idea why, and I have even spent a little bit of time trying to figure out what it would cost to do this. It turns out to be prohibitively expensive, especially once one adds in the snacks, toys, and so forth that each child would need in the shipping box. I would never box them up and ship them to Timbuktu without snacks. That would be cruel.

Sometimes "If you don't empty this dishwasher right now I am going to box you up and FedEx you to Timbuktu" takes too long to say. It lacks directness. It allows the child being threatened too much time to escape and clap some headphones on their head as a plausible reason to say "What, Mom? Sorry, I didn't hear ya!" Therefore, the threat gets shortened to "Get in the box." This can be delivered as "Get. In. The BOX" if you need it to sound especially emphatic. If you're a bit rushed, you can just look them in the eyes and simply say "Box."

Kaiden had a pretty clever idea for a Halloween costume this year consisting of a FedEx box upon which was written a bunch of really dumb things in Sharpie. Of course, we began with "TO: TIMBUKTU" because it's always Timbuktu. Following that we had a good time writing things like "Schrodinger's Box: Live Animals (Or Are They?)" and "This End Up, Or Death Awaits You," which was naturally upside down. A lot of people didn't understand that costume at all, but sophistication at our level is hard to find.

Jayce: BOX!

"Get in the box" is one of the things we Price kids all understand. When we are all driving Mom out of her mind, she says to get in the box. It is understood that she would never FedEx me anywhere without my snacks, so I will have one FedEx truck for me and one for my snacks.

When we're driving down the road somewhere and we see a FedEx truck we all make a big goofy scene and holler "Uh oh, who is the truck picking up this time?"

Kelly: Go The Fuck To School, Work, Therapy, and Sleep

None of the above items are optional for any kid in the house unless child labor laws preclude the "work" part. Even then, I can find chores for them to do. I routinely pray for somebody to misbehave because when they do it means I get my van cleaned. I figure this means either way I get something good, either well behaved children who don't scream a lot or a nice clean vehicle that doesn't smell like feet. I can't have both, apparently, but I've chosen to believe that is not a problem.

School, it should go without saying, is the main job in their lives, because school will ultimately render them educated enough to live independently and maybe even take care of me extremely well when I am old, next week.

Therapy is also a major obligation for every Price child. Four out of four of them are in some form of therapy. They all need someplace to process the bullshit inherent in their lives and they need somebody other than me who can determine whether they are crazy in a way that requires intervention. This brings me to a recent anecdote.

Jayce was feeling out of control again and had reverted to old patterns of coping with emotional upheaval; to wit: digging holes in his skin with pointy things. He is aware on an intellectual level that digging holes in his skin with pointy things is not the safest or most desirable way of coping, but it's quick and for some reason he is constantly surrounded by pointy things. If instead of being adopted by our family he'd been adopted by a prickle of porcupines he would still be less surrounded by pointy things than he is now. And yes, a group of porcupines is called a prickle. I learned it on Twitter.

This necessitated another trip to the crisis center to get a clinician to look him over and decide whether or not he was safe to be at home and what the next plan should be. We actually set out at the relatively civilized hour of about eight at night as opposed to our traditional 1:00 am arrival time.

When we got there this nice nurse came into the triage room, looked us over, and said "You two were here like a week ago, right?"

Nope. Ten *months ago*, to be exact. This, perhaps predictably, caused us to begin giggling like idiots.

"They see people in here who have all kinds of horrifying circumstances, suicidal people, hallucinating people, people with DTs, and WE are what they remember??! And not only that but the last ten months without us have apparently been a blur!" We found this hysterically funny. As usual, laughing about it made him feel better and after some assessment and some counseling he felt well enough to come home and get some sleep.

Jayce: The rules are not that damn hard.

"Go the fuck to work, school, sleep, and therapy." These are the most basic rules I have to follow, and there's really not much more. They came from Samuel L. Jackson's online reading of a book called "Go The Fuck To Sleep" that is hilarious. Mom says I have to get educated so I can date cute, smart girls. You have to go to therapy so your cute, smart girlfriend doesn't have to deal with your traumatized ass so much, and you gotta go to work so you can support yourself so the cute, smart girl doesn't have to feed you. Going to sleep lets you go to work. Generally that's all you need. Work, school, sleep, and therapy.

If you think about it, Mom says these things out of love, but really it's mostly all about her.

Chapter 30
Kelly: TransGear – Binders and Packers and Gadgets, Oh My

The majority of Americans have some kind of gadget they use or wear to make life a little easier. It doesn't matter if you have a mobility issue, a sensory thing, or a cosmetic thing, the odds are very good that you have something you need to keep yourself functional and comfortable.

The array of available gizmos is a large one. You can buy a wheelchair that climbs stairs and raises you to standing height, custom prosthetic limbs that are 3D printed to fit the wearer exactly, walkers, scooters, robotic vacuum cleaners, the list goes on and on.

Eyeball prosthetics come to mind as the most commonly used apparatus of this type. I am not talking about glass eyes, although those are fascinating by themselves, and the desire to own a large number of them that could be used as beads on a necklace or inserted into holes in a wall and backlit for an extremely creepy effect at Halloween has come over me. I am actually referring to something much more pedestrian, though—glasses and contacts.

Before the advent of LASIK surgery I had an eyeglass prescription of -9 diopters in one eye and -10.5 in the other. I was very, very impaired without glasses, to the point of disability. I was also astigmatic as hell. This made life very challenging if I didn't have access to my glasses, as occurred one day in San Francisco.

The weather was glorious that day, hot and with bright sun, which is unusual for the Bay Area. I packed a basket of snacks and a towel, threw on a bathing suit under my clothes, and headed for Ocean Beach on the bus.

The ocean temperature of the Pacific in that particular stretch of coastline ranges from about 53 to about 60 degrees Fahrenheit. If you're in water that is in that range you've got a survival time of about 1-6 hours before hypothermia kills you off. So yes, you can swim there, but it's not balmy and tropical, it's more bracing and refreshing, which is a nice way of saying you will freeze your ass off. Anecdotal evidence from scuba divers in the area south of San Francisco near Monterey indicates that at some point while diving there most divers will decide to pee in their wetsuits for the elusive and temporary feeling of warmth it brings. I myself have no clue whether this is true, so if you have done this... go ahead and keep it to yourself.

Anyway, I decided that if swimming wasn't an option, wading certainly was, and I went out to about knee depth in the sea, enjoying the contrast between the bright warm sun and the cold water.

I turned around to wave at a friend on the beach and WHAM, got smacked in the back of the head by a big wave that seemed to come from nowhere. It knocked me over, tossed me around a bit for good measure, and then receded. I got my feet under me at last and stood up... and realized I couldn't see. I ducked back down and frantically felt around near my feet in hopes that by some miracle my spectacles had ended up someplace close by, but to no avail. The ocean had claimed them and swallowed them whole. They had been taken by King Neptune as sacrifice for my love of crab legs and clam chowder.

I floundered back to the beach, where I quickly realized that I not only couldn't find where my towel and basket (and friend!) had been left, I couldn't even tell which street I was near. I could tell a building from a tree, but could not find the door to said building. Figuring out which bus I needed to board to get home was suddenly a much more challenging task than it had been before.

Eventually, and with a lot of assistance from random colorful blobs I assumed to be people, I got home. I couldn't work until I had new glasses, and I had to have a friend take me to the eye clinic to get them. Shopping for groceries was impossible. Reading and watching TV were an absolute fail. Until I got new glasses, I was bored, blind, hungry, and unemployed.

Transgender people also use tools and equipment to help manage their gender dysphoria so that their daily lives are easier. The coping methods trans people choose to use are as varied as the people themselves. What works for one person might well not work at all for another. Treating gender dysphoria is an extremely individualized process and relies upon a relationship between the client and the practitioners providing care. Some people use medications and equipment to deliver those medications, like hormone shots. Others seek out surgical procedures to help bring their bodies more into line with their knowledge of their gender identity. There are also items sold that help to make people's bodies look and function the way the owners perceive that they should. Here I am going to try to give the reader some straightforward advice about what is available and how it might be used. Be reminded that my expertise on gear for the transgender woman is much less extensive than that for the transgender man. I'm also going to reiterate that wherever you are on the gender spectrum, there is likely something that can be done to make you feel more like your body and your self are in accord. You need to make your decisions with support from a qualified healthcare team who are thoroughly familiar with your personal situation. So, without further ado, here we go.

Medications

Medications for treating gender dysphoria include hormonal and nonhormonal drugs and the delivery systems used to administer them. You can get puberty blockers that delay the onset of adolescent changes to give kids more time to figure things out, androgens (for men) and estrogens (for women) that cause physiological changes such as hair growth, breast development, changes to someone's voice, and so forth. Some medications are expensive, some aren't. Some require shots, some can be delivered via skin patches, and some can be taken orally. One thing that is true for every single one of these meds, though, is that none of them are dosed in megaliters.

We all love those little computer voices that answer pharmacy calls, don't we? We call to refill a medication and the little voice goes "Please enter your prescription number." That number will be fifteen digits long and written in tiny print, and if you mistype as you are squinting at it your day will get just that much longer when the computerized voice in the phone goes "Please enter a valid prescription number."

When we call in Jayce's testosterone prescription we eventually get to the voice saying "This prescription is: Testosteronecyp200mg/ml1**megaliter**28daysupply" all in one word. That "Megaliter" thing is kinda hidden in there, which is why I point it out to you. Why nobody has caught and changed it in the recording is a mystery, given how unrealistic it would be to expect insurance to pay for it.

One megaliter of testosterone is the same as one million liters and is equal to about 264,172 gallons. The average level of testosterone for a man is about 679 nanograms per deciliter of blood, so for an average guy we're talking about 3.2×10^{-5} grams of testosterone. A megaliter, therefore, would contain enough testosterone to adequately fuel the "dude, hold my beer" tendencies of about 335,000,000,000 dudes of average dudeliness. Not only would Jayce need a syringe the size of the Empire State Building for this, taking the shot would require a LOT of determination. He should really be able to open the pickles afterward, though.

Binders

A binder is sort of like the equivalent of shapewear for a trans guy. The object of the binder is to reduce chest dysphoria by making the contours of a trans guy's chest appear more masculine. If you have experimented with shapewear you are probably relatively familiar with how comfortable, cool, and easy-to-wear these garments... aren't. They take parts of your body that have been freely taking up space in the universe and mash them into an unfamiliar shape and position by dint of sheer brute force and the power of Spandex. You cannot do the most basic things in a shapewear garment, and eating, breathing, and peeing all start to seem like luxuries you just can't afford. You cannot WAIT to come home from whatever event required you to squash yourself into these things and peel them off.

The peeling-off process is also a royal pain. There are YouTube videos out there that will show you how to get out of your binder. Watch them before you try it yourself, because it's hard to watch a video with your arms securely bound above your head by an impenetrable layer of Spandex that is also covering your face.

Now imagine that in order to feel enough like yourself to function in the outside world, you need to wear one of these things every single day. Doesn't matter if it's ninety degrees and 80% humidity, you somehow have to get yourself into a binder, wear it all day without ending up as an irritable, obnoxious monster, hand wash the thing, and do it all again the next day... for years on end. Furthermore, you need them in different colors and styles, because putting a black binder on under a white men's dress shirt is guaranteed to get you some unwanted attention.

TransTape

This stuff is a lot like the kind of tape physical therapists use to support injured body parts, except wider and flesh-toned. It does come in a bunch of different colors that match a variety of skin tones. It is also designed to help manage chest dysphoria, and it is to the binder what the stick-on strapless bra is to the shapewear. A lot of trans guys swear by this stuff, it makes them look the way they want to look even when they aren't wearing shirts.

When I was a lactating mother after I had Kaiden, my bra cup size went to a G-cup. (Daniel said this stood for "GodDAMN!") I couldn't see my feet. If you stood close to me I couldn't see your feet either. Things are better in that respect now, but I still have a lot of difficulty imagining what it would be like to secure those sensitive parts of my anatomy into my armpits with lots and lots of super strong tape. I have even more difficulty imagining what it would be like to *remove* lots and lots of super strong tape from those areas of my skin. You can buy adhesive-remover wipes at the grocery store, and four hundred or so of the little wipes would probably do the job, but it'd be better to just buy it by the vat from your neighborhood medical supply store.

Thinx, Lunapads, Periods, and Dudes

Thinx and Lunapads are a relatively new line of products that fit into a category called "period underwear." When I was a teenager the phrase "period underwear" meant your oldest, ugliest granny panties, the ones with the fortitude to hold eighteen inches of absorbent pads (with wings!) in a position that ensured that when you were changing for PE class at school everybody in the locker room knew you were in Hell Week. These are better. There are actually a bunch of brands, but these two are the ones I know of that have specifically considered the needs of trans guys. You can wear them as a replacement for regular underwear along with other feminine hygiene products, or you can just wear them alone. They are extremely absorbent, leakproof, tight fitting, and reviewers say they're comfortable, washable, and look and feel like regular underwear. These two brands make their underwear in a tight-fitting boxer short style that can be a godsend for a trans guy whose physiology insists upon behaving like that of a woman entirely against his will. Since my physiology does the same damn thing and has since I was thirteen years old, I share some of their resentment, but my own challenges in that respect aren't much compared to living with periods AND gender dysphoria. Any guy who can tolerate this shit deserves a lifetime supply of chocolate. Period.

Packers

I would like to apologize to Green Bay football fans, because if you read this chapter you're not really gonna be able to un-learn this stuff. It's relevant, it's important, and it will help treat the damn dysphoria for a trans male kid, so roll with me, it's worth it.

Long ago when I was in fifth grade, my class got to learn about sex as part of our unit on the human body. A whole gaggle of wriggling, mortified ten-year-old kids sat in the classroom waiting to be hideously embarrassed by our teachers and trying desperately to hide behind our notebooks and desks in an effort to avoid being called on at any time during this unit. Most of us knew something about reproductive anatomy from an external point of view, and none of us could imagine a more hellish fate than being asked to describe these things in detail.

My teacher at that time was a kind lady named Mrs. Darcy who was a veteran educator. She knew that getting us past the mental squirming we were all doing required serious intervention, and so she stood in front of the room one day and made us all repeat the word "Penis" until it lost all meaning. You have not lived until you have sat in a fifth grade classroom on a cold April afternoon going "Penis penis penis penis penis" for three or four solid minutes. Eventually the word simply loses its power to shock. It becomes just another body part, and then you can move on to the next topic. If you need to do that now, put the book down and say the word until you feel better.

Transgender guys are faced with choices for modification of their genitalia that are pretty damn daunting. They're offered expensive, complicated surgeries like phalloplasty, which takes tissue from other parts of the body to construct a penis, and metoidioplasty, which uses the patient's own clitoris to create a penis after enlargement with hormones. A scrotum with prosthetic testicles can then be constructed from the labia. Sounds like fun, doesn't it? Having a bunch of very complex and delicate body structures modified this way carries some risks,

285

including permanent urinary and sexual dysfunctions, so a lot of guys elect to skip these procedures entirely.

Fortunately, there are devices available that act as prosthetic penises, and these are referred to as packers. They're generally made from body safe materials like silicone and they're designed to sit against the body at the same position as a penis on a cisgender male. They can also be made at home from such simple things as a pair of socks or nylons rolled to fit into underwear.

Packer technology hasn't quite caught up with the rest of the prosthetics world for sure. You can't get a computerized 3D printed schlong that interfaces with your brain waves. They don't interact with your smartphone. There isn't an app for that. You can't get one that lights up so you can see to pee in the middle of the night. However, it IS possible to get packers that will allow the wearer to 1.) look like a cisgender guy in a pair of shorts, 2.) urinate standing up, and 3.) have sex. Yes, really.

There are a couple of caveats to this, though. The first issue is that trans guys, like most other guys, often have an overinflated sense of what SIZE packer they need.

"Big, Mom," a trans teen boy will say, pointing to a photo of a product called the Happy Stallion in some online catalog. "The biggest one. That one." Mom, who very likely has some experience with real world penises, will gently try to guide her enthusiastic son in the direction of something a bit more modest. Sometimes this even works.

Another issue inherent in packer use is that you really have to have a way to secure the packer in position so that it will not migrate down your pant leg and into your sock or fall out on the men's room floor. Different gadgets for this purpose include special underwear with rings and harnesses to hold the packer secure, plain old boxer briefs with a pouch in the front, and fabric pouches that can be pinned to any pair of underwear.

Leaving the packer lying around for just anyone to find can also result in some interesting household conversations, especially when a younger sibling—or the dog—locates the item and decides it's a special new toy, or when Grandma comes to visit and finds an apparently disembodied penis lying on a bedroom floor. If you've got more than one trans guy living in your house I suppose it would also be possible to mix them up, resulting in the need for willy tattoos done with Sharpies.

If you buy the right kind of packer you can also use it as an STP, or stand-to-pee device. This is one form of penis envy that a lot of cisgender women relate to as well, particularly those who like to camp or attend music festivals with disgusting porta-potties. This is not to say that women specifically seek out music festivals with disgusting porta-potties, just that any porta-potty within 500 yards of a music festival has to pass a test to show that it is properly equipped with wet toilet paper wads, beer cans, cigarette butts, and assorted bodily effluvia of the kinds of people who attend music festivals. They make a variety of gadgets girls can use for this purpose, but these tend to be pink or lavender and have names like "Go Girl" and "Shewee" which might be a little bit dysphoria-triggering to a trans guy.

These kinds of packers do have an obvious pitfall. Managing to get all the pee into the toilet/urinal/tall weeds and none of it into your shoes requires a little bit of dexterity and practice, and it is highly recommended that a trans guy trying to learn the ropes practice in the shower until he's comfortable (with and without clothing) and then at home before taking the act on the road. Moms of trans boys (or indeed any boys) should therefore keep their bathrooms well stocked with disinfectant wipes and inform all male members of the household that leaving things better than you found them is a virtue.

I mentioned back there that it's actually possible to get a packer you can use for sex, too. There is a company called Transthetics that is run by a transgender guy named Alex, an avid athlete with the brain of a structural engineer and a lot of trans friends to beta test his ideas. (A running joke around here is that if my trans dudes ever got the urge to send dick pics to somebody all they'd have to do would be link to the Transthetics catalog.) Some of the different items out there include packers with vibrating inserts so that both partners can have enjoyable sex and very user-friendly STP devices, but the coolest thing he is working on now is something called the Bionic. This gizmo is the Cadillac of penis prosthetics and is designed to work as authentically as it possibly can.

Unfortunately, there have been some delays in production and development for a number of reasons, but both the University of Denver and the Colorado School of Mines have gotten on board. With all those minds working on the project, it will be spectacular when it does arrive on the scene. Features to be added include skin that looks, feels, and moves like real skin, vibrators and erection functions that are controlled either by remote control or by pelvic floor muscles, and a way to secure it to the body with implantable magnets. It will be the only willy on the market with servomotors and hydraulics. They're exploring the possibility of linking it to a fitness tracker that will trigger an erection if it detects an increase in heart rate, with an override to prevent too much enthusiasm from happening every time a guy goes for a jog.

I was so impressed with this thing that I emailed Alex and offered my services as part of his US medical sales team. Being an RN I work with people all the time who use prosthetics and a packer is no different from any other medical device. I've got some acquired credibility due to being a middle-aged nurse and mom of transgender babies that I'm prepared to mobilize, because making my kids' lives easier is important.

All these tools have the potential to help our trans kids live as comfortably in their bodies as the privileged cisgender class. Their use should be as normal for trans people as glasses are for the nearsighted Bat People among us.

Jayce: You can do something about the dysphoria. This is HUGE.

If you're transgender you most likely have to cope with and battle with gender dysphoria on a daily basis, and let me tell you, it's a bitch. Before I was treated with hormones and surgical modifications, I would describe it as being enclosed in a box where cockroaches are climbing all over you. As soon as you swat one away there's another one. You're just covered in cockroaches. It feels awful. Maybe it's not cockroaches, it could be snakes, but regardless it's something you hate. You go look in the mirror and you think you're happy with yourself but there's just something that's not right, and whatever your body looks like or however you see yourself, to you it's just not as good as it could be. It's so unsatisfying. Other people perceive it in different ways but this is how it feels to me.

The treatment for gender dysphoria is transition, and it is considered a medical diagnosis. It was formerly lumped in with mental health, but although it definitely affects your mental health it's medical.

One treatment option is hormone replacement therapy, which means you put yourself through a second puberty and you start developing secondary sex characteristics that match the gender you identify with. For men, you take testosterone. For women you'd take estrogen. I don't know as much about estrogen as I do about T, but anyhow when you're roughly 14 or older you can go on gender affirming hormones, and affirming your gender makes you feel so much better.

If you're younger than that, like maybe 7 or 8, you can go on something called puberty blockers. Those can delay adolescent changes until a kid can figure stuff out. They might decide to continue with their biological puberty or to go on hormone replacement therapy, but at least they have the time to make the decision instead of just suffering through whatever puberty biology has in store for them.

For me, testosterone therapy changed my life. I didn't know how much I needed it until I started taking injections, but as soon as I did day by day I felt more confident. I don't have to get my hair cut every two weeks or wear my hat backward anymore, because I feel more like myself and I can just let some things go. It's nice to feel like a guy even if my hair touches my ears.

The other thing most trans guys do is bind their chest. A binder is like an elastic tank top you use to bind the breast tissue, to give your chest a flatter appearance. This is what many people do before they get top surgery, and most people who bind do eventually get surgery. A lot of people complain that binding is very uncomfortable. I can't speak for everybody, but for me I never thought it was too tight or that I couldn't breathe in it. You do need to be conscious of binding safety, because you can put yourself at risk for injury due to the tight fit of the binders, but for me it was worth it to treat the dysphoria. Until I got top surgery I had no problem binding but since I've gotten surgery I can't figure out how I ever coped with that for two or three years of my life.

An alternative to binding is something called trans tape. It's an invention by a trans guy, similar to the KT tape that physical therapists use. You use it to stretch and flatten the breast tissue and give you a flatter appearance. A lot of people like this because some people can go shirtless in public before they can get surgery, and others can do it just around the house. Trans Tape doesn't work for all body types. I tried it but it is something that takes practice. It was okay for me, and when my surgery date got postponed I had planned to start taping again. It was something I didn't do on a daily basis, but then I fortunately got scheduled for a surgery date. So I ended up giving my tape away to someone else who needed it.

One thing you need to know about Trans Tape is that getting it on and off is quite a task so you'd better have someone in your family who can help you. You don't want to damage your skin, especially if you have an upcoming top surgery.

Some trans guys also use packers. A packer is a prosthetic penis that resembles the male anatomy, and it can serve different purposes. A lot of people use them to feel more confident with that part of their body, because bottom surgery is very extensive. You can spend 1-2 years of your life recovering from it, and it is multiple stages. If you can find something temporary that helps you cope, that's fine. I luckily don't have a ton of bottom dysphoria, I have some but I can get by day to day and I don't think my lower anatomy defines me any less as a guy.

One advantage trans guys have over cisgender guys is the ability to adjust their packer selection to the occasion they're using it for. If it needs to vibrate on a hot date, it can. If it needs to let you use a men's room inconspicuously it can do that too. You can have a wardrobe of willies for all different purposes instead of just having to work with the one you were born with.

Another advantage is that you can do sports without one at all if you want to, which makes things like rock climbing harnesses a lot more comfortable.

I am very fortunate to have completed my transition; I have gotten on hormones and gotten top surgery. For people struggling with really debilitating dysphoria, there are things you can use to cope and you do have the right to be comfortable in your own body.

This is easier said than done, but the little things add up over time and you can work your way toward feeling the way you want to.

Chapter 31

Kelly: Adventures in Plastic Surgery

One of the questions trans people get that brings eye rolls and a cynical snort is "So, have you had The Surgery yet?" The phrase "Sex change" is an outdated one and implies that a single miraculous operation can deliver a trans person the body he's always wanted but wasn't born in. My trans kids and their friends are forever envisioning an emporium of body parts where you could drop off superfluous breasts and pick up a penis and testicles on a sort of BOGO deal. Like trading in a car, you could test drive them to make sure they work correctly and that the stick shift engages the transmission and the thing doesn't leak. You could then return them if they don't have enough legroom or the vanity mirrors are too small and you bought the three day right-to-return policy. And now you are picturing a penis with a vanity mirror, aren't you? You're welcome.

"The Surgery," for a trans guy, actually consists of several different operations. "Top surgery," or bilateral mastectomy with chest masculinization, metoidioplasty (creation of a penis from a clitoris enlarged by hormones), phalloplasty (creation of a penis from other grafted body tissues), and hysterectomy with removal of Fallopian tubes and ovaries are all options. Which choices a guy might make are highly individual and need to be made with the help of a discerning, experienced team, but all of them are major surgeries and some are done in more than one stage. A guy seeking transition can do all or none of these procedures. If he needs to do all of them, he's going to lose a substantial chunk of his life in recovering and waiting for the next one. It is one hell of a process even if everything goes perfectly.

For Jayce a major source of his dysphoria was his chest, and so he was understandably delighted when he got put on the operating room schedule for top surgery at the University of Colorado in April 2020. We did a little happy dance and then Jayce started following everyone around going "This will happen, right? This is real? What should I expect? I'm not gonna die, am I?" and generally driving everyone bugfuck. I, on the other hand, started trying to improve his nutrition, figure out how to get him to take his vitamins, and plan for what we'd need to keep him clean, infection free, and healthy postoperatively.

Then COVID-19 hit and all bets were suddenly off. The news filled with terrible pictures of sobbing healthcare workers and stories of overrun hospitals and morgues. The entire world went into lockdown in an effort to contain the pandemic, with variable effectiveness. Virtual graduations, birthday parades, and playdates became the new norm. Three weeks prior to Jayce's surgery date University Hospital cancelled all elective procedures, and a devastated Jayce geared up to spend another summer in a binder or tape and we all figured it would be autumn - if he was lucky - before he could get the procedure done.

We finished the semester in a bewildering whirlwind of baked goods, Zoom meetings, malfunctioning computer learning platforms, and uncertainty. I went a tiny bit nuts and impulse-bought fifty pounds of wheat, which when combined with a crank grain mill and a breezy day covers me in flour from head to toe. We planted a garden, learned some new crafts, and started making a plan for the summer, and then suddenly in mid-May the call came saying that Jayce could get his procedure done that month.

Jayce was nervous about the operation, which meant that he was by turns irritable, obnoxious, snippy, bossy, and stubborn. We broke up sibling fights, delivered lectures about how not to be an utter jerk, offered reassurance that since he's young and healthy he could expect to heal just fine, cooked double portions of a bunch of different recipes so we'd have stuff to eat while he recovered, and waited for his day to finally come.

He was scheduled for the first time slot on that day, which required that we check in at the hospital by 5:30 in the morning. He was also supposed to shower and drink some clear liquids around 3:30 am, so he got up, did all that, and then we hung out until it was time to leave, imagining what it would be like to try to teach an ostrich named Marvin to play the drums. Why, nobody knows, but the image of an ostrich beating a drum with its head had both of us in stitches, and so we took our lunacy to the preop area and got checked in right on time.

Because of the pandemic, I was relegated to waiting in the check in area in a face mask for the duration. This was a large uncomfortable beige room, and by beige room I mean that the furniture was beige, the carpets were beige, the walls were beige, and the artwork was, you guessed it, beige. Somebody got a fleet discount at some carpet factory on acres and acres of light beige rug with a dark beige stripe. I pictured an employee in this place trying to give directions to a lost visitor and going "Well look, you go down the beige hallway to the beige door, walk through that into the other beige hallway, and you should see a lady in beige at a check in desk there. You can't miss her. If you see some color that isn't beige though you're outside, so turn around and come back in." I waited until they took him back and then went down to the cafeteria for a breakfast of entirely beige food.

They also have this awesome system there for communicating with you about how your loved one is doing via text message. You get these personal, reassuring messages like "The patient is in the operating room." "The procedure has begun." "The procedure is progressing." Eventually you get one that reads "The patient is in recovery." After this you can then expect a call from either the surgeon or the recovery room nurse or both telling you what the scoop is and how things are going, and having a conversation with an actual human being will seem fabulous by that point. We were

297

lucky because since I am an RN I felt completely comfortable with postoperative care and monitoring, but there was another mom in there who seemed totally overwhelmed by her son's care needs. When in the hospital it is considerate to avoid too much aggressive eavesdropping on other people's clinical situations, but it's hard to miss someone in a public hallway whose voice is steadily rising past anxiety into hysteria as she goes "Drains. DRAINS. I had no idea he'd have drains! I DON'T KNOW HOW TO DEAL WITH DRAINS!" I felt bad enough for the lady that I offered to answer questions for her, an idea that she rejected with a clipped "NO, thank you" and a resolute forward stare with lips pressed into a thin white line. I figured oh well, I tried, and left her to it.

Jayce stayed steady as a rock through the entire operation, spent an anticlimactic couple of hours in recovery, came home feeling pretty good, and seemed to bounce back flawlessly. He was already aware that being allowed to fester in his own filth with no monitoring was not going to be an option for him, so he had to put up with a lot of bullshit from me in the form of Dude Wipes and digital thermometers and maternal hovering. A few days later, about the time I quit hovering so much, we were standing in the bathroom doing routine drain care (there's the damn drains again) and Jayce got really quiet and then went pale and his eyes rolled up in his head.

So much for independence and a complication-free recovery, right?

I got him down to the floor without grievously injuring either of us and checked his blood pressure. Low. Not "imminent death" low, but "not quite adequate to maintain consciousness in an upright position" low. Delivery of restorative medicine in the form of root beer and graham crackers failed to elicit the desired response, so we called 911 and some nice paramedics came and loaded Jayce into an ambulance and turned him into a pincushion trying to get an IV while they drove him to our local emergency room.

Here is one of those places where being transgender colors circumstances. My kid, whose name, ID, and own voice indicate he's male, had just gone through a bilateral mastectomy. Extra communication was needed between the paramedics on the road and the ER about why a boy of twenty had required a mastectomy. Furthermore, as mom to a trans kid you get kind of wary and mistrustful because you hear a lot of horror stories about terrible care and mean people who refuse to help them in the bathroom and people who want to know what's in your child's pants when they show up with an eye infection. In our society, transgender kids are at risk simply by virtue of being transgender. COVID-19 had severely restricted visiting policies in hospitals, but once I told the security people that my child was postoperative and trans they decided they wanted to know where I was instead of having me wandering around making trouble (wise!) and allowed me back in the room with him.

I could tell he was starting to feel better within a couple of hours. Early symptoms of returning health included badgering his mother with questions about whether or not this whole thing had been really necessary. When informed by both myself and his nurse that a 911 call and an ambulance ride were entirely reasonable given his condition, he ignored us completely and texted Michelle (the medically untrained photographer) for confirmation. This satisfied him. Sheesh.

Things continued to improve to the point that he started doing another fun thing he'd been doing since he came out of surgery. This consisted of either patting himself on the chest, peering down the neck of his shirt, or both, reassuring himself that nothing he'd had removed had grown back, and going "Yay!" a lot. He was delighted at being allowed to lie there shirtless while receiving treatment. Swathed in bandages from neck to knees and with his drain tubes clipped to a pink lanyard, but shirtless. Being shirtless has been a thing he was looking forward to in a big way, so putting on a shirt to him felt like a step backward.

In my haste to get to the hospital I had completely forgotten to bring the boy any clothes to wear home. He had on boxer shorts that passed pretty well as regular shorts, but not much else. He did have a pair of those very attractive slipper socks with the nonskid soles, but no shoes either.

'Hmm…" said the nurse. "Do you want me to get you a scrub top to go home in or something?"

Jayce thought about it for a second, looked down and did his "Yay!" thing, and then said "Nah, screw it, I'm good."

I want you all to close your eyes and imagine a skinny kid clad only in underwear and sexy hospital socks (beige) with bandages on both hands, both elbows, and across his chest, and also wearing a hot pink lanyard with a couple of drains clipped to it. Now add me to the picture – fiftyish hippie type with a homemade tie dye on, helping the aforementioned kid across the parking lot. If your mental image was created correctly you will now understand why the security guard came out of the ER urgently saying "Um, excuse me? EXCUSE ME?! Can I see your wrists?"

I looked Jayce up and down from messy hair to sexy socks and thought wow, this is the picture you're taking in, and the thing you want to see most are his wrists. Mmmm-kay. And because we are what we are we were both instantly paralyzed with hilarity. It's a good thing it didn't hurt to laugh. We hooted and whooped our way to McDonald's, (hey, the kid was ravenous) where the lady in the drive thru window took one look into our car, handed us our order, and closed the window *reallyfast*. COVID-19 is contagious, but being trans, half naked, crazy, and postoperative is not. We laughed our asses off the whole way home. Daniel looked Jayce over when we got home and said "Dude. Did they get you high?"

"Nope," said Jayce. "Just me."

His operation was a fabulous success, he looks amazing. Masculine and happy. The joy on his face as he looked in the mirror after the bandages came off was worth ALL of the bullshit.

Jayce: Permanently Shirtless. Yay!

As I started to treat my dysphoria and get things accomplished for my transition, things got easier and easier. Things like getting my name changed and testosterone had gotten done and now I was ready to address one of my biggest transition goals, which was top surgery. I never thought this was going to happen, it was something I thought was at least five years off. My former parents discouraged my transition process completely. I was always told that if I got on testosterone I'd become more aggressive and be kicked out, or that I had to wait till age 25 to get surgery.

Fortunately, when I landed with the Prices one of their top priorities was helping me get my transition completed. We spoke to a couple of different surgeons and finally met a doctor we liked. I was ready to get this thing on the road. We thought that once I got put on the operating room schedule things would be great, but of course there just had to be bullshit. At first, I was scheduled for the middle of March, but the scheduler screwed it up and my doctor had a conflict, so they pushed me back to April 6. That sucked, but we figured no big deal, we'd just wait a few more weeks.

Then COVID-19 hit and the hospitals cancelled all elective procedures. It absolutely sucked to get that call saying my surgery was cancelled. Mom and Dad could see it coming and tried to prepare me, and it was a responsible decision and the hospital did all the right things, but it sucked nonetheless. So, I was prepared to bind and tape and go through the summer hoping for September or October to get back on the schedule. I was surprised and very happy to get a call May 13 to say I could get in on May 28.

The day finally came, and I was so nervous. The two weeks prior to surgery were among the hardest in my life. I was nervous because one, I'd never had a surgery like this or gone under anesthesia, and two I was trying to mentally prepare myself for having it cancelled again. I had no idea if we were gonna make it those two weeks. Mom kept telling me I would be just fine and that she was going to take care of me, but the waiting and the anxiety were incredibly hard to cope with.

I had to be there at 5:30 am on the day of surgery, and so I got up at 3:30 and followed all my presurgical instructions like getting a drink of Gatorade and taking a shower. I had never been happier to get up at 3:30 in the morning. Mom and I drove to the hospital and the reality finally hit, I was really here, I had made it. I was finally having surgery. For the weeks and months beforehand I had been looking at so many pictures of trans guys on Instagram and thinking when will it be my turn, and here I finally was.

Just like any other morning with my mom, we were laughing and being idiots, and the waiting room was incredibly beige and we were laughing about who might make beige artwork. The poor guy across from us in the waiting room had to be thinking "What the hell are these people doing at 5 am, I gotta go sit somewhere else," but he never did. Mom wasn't allowed to go back with me to the preop area or sit with me in recovery because of the pandemic, but the staff were wonderful. They got me going right on time, I got relaxed, and I woke up flat, sore, and happy.

I recovered really well. I was way ahead of the curve. About four days later, though, I keeled over on Mom in the bathroom during a normal routine emptying of the drains. I was just standing there by the sink and suddenly I felt nauseated, and I couldn't tell where my mom's voice was coming from, and I was just tilting over.

Then I ended up down on the floor and she said I had passed out. I had to go to the ER, which I didn't think was necessary, but oh well.

My mom said "Hey Kaiden, go flag down the paramedics," and Kaiden (who had been upstairs and had no idea what was going on) was like "What the hell happened?"

That ambulance ride was no fun. I had never complained about needles before but when they stuck this huge spike in my arm it felt like an electrical shock went down my arm. I was so dehydrated they had to stick me like four times to get the IV in, and my mom said later that they had to put in a big IV line to get me rehydrated quickly.

A few hours later I was rehydrated, still covered in bandages, wearing my drains on my hot pink lanyard (which you need so the drains don't just dangle.) I was over the moon because I was lying there NOT in a gown, but shirtless. Dehydrated and semiconscious or not I knew I didn't want to wear a shirt.

When the security guard flagged us down as we walked out; we must have been an interesting sight. I was thinking okay, is he gonna tell me to go back in and put clothes on or ask "Hey, are you aware you're not wearing anything?" But all he said was "Let me see your wrists." That was such a weird thing for him to ask for that true to form my mom and I burst out laughing.

I was hungry, I hadn't eaten for hours, and so we went to McDonald's. I told Mom on the way there not to get pulled over so we didn't have to explain why she had a mostly undressed, bandaged kid in the car to the cops and end up in a hospital and a jail in the same day.

We finally made it home and I walked into the house still laughing like an idiot.

That was the only bullshit we had to contend with as far as surgery recovery. Dad was super happy when I recovered enough so I could mow the lawn again.

There is no better feeling than finally getting to look down at my chest and see me, the way I am meant to be. My transition is completed, I have friends, I'm educated, my family loves me, and it has all been worth it. I would do it all over again in a second, bullshit and all.

Chapter 32

Kelly: Gotcha Day

Adopting a child is a really exciting event. Whether you do a private adoption, an international adoption, or an adoption from foster care, the day you actually finalize the adoption and make the little monkey in your heart into an official legal member of your family is the culmination of something big.

As a result, a lot of families with adopted kids celebrate Gotcha Day, logically and obviously defined as the day they Gotcha.

Our family tends to do Gotcha Day as an experiential sort of family day. We don't go in for gifts and it isn't a huge ostentatious affair, we just let the Gotcha Day Kid choose someplace they want to go to eat or do something fun as a family.

Kaiden's Gotcha Day is a little different because we celebrate his on July 5, which was the day we brought him home from the hospital. It's more of a Gotcha Home Day. No matter how I tried

I couldn't quite get the neonatology team to let us bring Kaiden home on July 4, but we still tell him every year that the fireworks are just for him. July 5 we sometimes go out to eat or sometimes let Kaiden choose something else he wants to do, and we all go together to be happy that we have Kaiden and that he has turned out completely awesome despite having grown up with me as his mother. He's warped, but he's awesome.

Gabrielle insisted for years that Gotcha Day was the day we should all go to Chuck E. Cheese. That particular restaurant chain has everything for the Gotcha Kid. Aside from an array of video games that dispense tickets to redeem for prizes worth 1/25 of a cent, it has Chuck E. himself, a nightmarish animatronic rat that clanks to life and plays music as part of a band of other similarly terrifying animals. I believe it is a rule that Chuck E. Cheese and his friends must always be in dire need of vacuuming. No sooner will Chuck E. and crew finish playing music than ANOTHER Chuck E., generally an underpaid teenager in a rodent suit that has seen better days, will appear at your table and pose for photos with all the children present. Children will hug him and pat him and sneeze on him and wipe pizza sauce on him. This proves that both real and fake rodents can be disease vectors, because we have quite literally never been to Chuck E. Cheese without one of the kids getting incredibly sick a week or so later.

Mari picks things that are practical, reasonably priced, and doable, which makes me think they are saving up their Gotcha Day Karma Points to ask for something really extravagant sometime in the future. This year they wanted to go to Costco and eat hot dogs. I am certain that Mari believes that Gotcha Day Karma Points are like Green Stamps and that they can be saved up to buy something really big. However, also like Green Stamps, they expire. When Mari looks up with big brown puppy eyes in a few years and asks if just this one time we can fly all their friends to Cancun for a Gotcha Day Weekend MariStravaganza, they are going to be terribly disappointed when we laugh airily at them and take them to Costco for hot dogs.

Jayce chose to go to Noodles & Company for his Gotcha Day this year. Not just any Noodles & Company, but THE Noodles & Company, the place where this crazy story all began. And so, we all piled into the van again and brought our tale around full circle to where it began.

Being inside that restaurant again was really surreal. The lady who had been our server for our first lunch wasn't there anymore. This was kind of a drag because I wanted a family photo with her in it. I wasn't sure whether I wanted the photo more as a souvenir of the anniversary or to see what her expression would look like when I said, "Excuse me, could you please join us for a photo, we ate here last year and ended up with a kid." I DID ask a random guy outside to take our picture in front of the doors, a request he may have found weird as hell but he went along with me anyway.

In that photo, we look absolutely, quintessentially like ourselves. It is painfully clear that this is no photo shoot with carefully curated outfits and neatly combed hair. The lighting is blinding and weird, the backdrop seems to be a random set of doors because our photographer didn't actually capture the Noodles & Company sign in the shot, and nobody is looking exactly where they are supposed to be. Mari's hair is completely covering their eyes and Daniel looks like he's soldiering through the day in spite of considerable pain. Our Gotcha Day photo captures a moment in time for a real family, a group of people united by mutual consent and circumstance instead of just by blood. A year has gone by, says this picture, and we are still cemented together, bonded by a whole lot... of bullshit.

Jayce: We All Got Each Other

I had heard the term "Gotcha Day" before, but it was never celebrated in my former household, even though I was adopted from Russia. I never knew much about my own adoption. Never saw my birth certificate or adoption paperwork. When I came to the Prices, I was surprised that anyone cared when, how, or why I came to the family. But I'll take it!

For my first Gotcha Day here we all went to the original Noodles & Company restaurant where I had met Kelly for lunch. This was the place where a year earlier, I essentially got a mom, a dad, and siblings. Going back there was a totally surreal experience, and of course it all still blows my mind. For my special day we had to have a family lunch where it all started and laugh about it. I ordered steak stroganoff, the same meal I had when we met there originally. My mom asked some random stranger to snap a family photo of all of us in front of the restaurant, which must have made him wonder what kind of weirdos we all were. However, we didn't want to re-create the entire Gotcha Day thing. If we had, we would have come home with another kid and my parents cannot afford that.

It was amazing to celebrate one year, and look back at everything I've gone through to get here, the people I met, and everything I've accomplished.

Chapter 33

Bullshit Managed

Well, for today anyway.

MEET THE AUTHORS

Kelly Price is a mom, wife, nurse, and activist who lives in Arvada, Colorado with her husband and kids. She enjoys hanging with her family and friends, playing sports badly, and working for her favorite causes.

Jayce Kennedy Price is a student, son, brother and friend. He enjoys anything to do with Avatar, music and dance, and sports that involve whacking things with other things (golf, racquetball, stuff like that.)